INFORMATION TECHNOLOGY

What's IT all about?

Colin Chapman
Advisory Teacher for Design & Technology

Val Charles
Advisory Teacher for Business Education

Mike Finney
Head of Technology,
William Farr C of E Comprehensive School, Welton

Michael Horsley
Advisory Teacher for Information Technology

Heather Jeffrey
Head of Home Economics,
King Edward VI School, Louth

Malcolm Moyes
Information Technology Coordinator,
Boston High School for Girls

CollinsEducational
An imprint of HarperCollins*Publishers*

Published in 1993 by CollinsEducational
An imprint of HarperCollins*Publishers*
77-85 Fulham Palace Road
Hammersmith
London W6 8JB

Colin Chapman, Val Charles, Mike Finney, Michael Horsley, Heather Jeffrey and Malcolm Moyes assert the moral right to be identified as the authors of this work.

ISBN 0 00 322063 X

Designed by Ken Vail Graphic Design,
(Production management Sally Moon)

Cover design by Raynor Design
Cover photograph by Chris Gilbert

Illustrated by James Alexander, Mike Lacey, courtesy of Simon Girling Associates, Tim Cooke, David Lock

School location photographs by Peter Sharp, Studio 7; and Nicola Cornish

Picture research by Caroline Mitchell

Printed and bound by Cambus Litho Limited

Commissioning Editor: Graham Bradbury
Project Editor: Alison Walters
Editor: Rebecca Lloyd
Production: Ken Ruskin

Note to teachers: This book is designed to inspire and inform. We have deliberately avoided specifying software because not all schools have the same IT resources. The IT Teacher's Guide (ISBN: 0 00 322065 6), however, contains details of relevant software.

WHAT'S THIS BOOK ABOUT?

In this book Information Technology (IT) is not a subject in itself. You are not being asked to go through the book page by page until you have finished. In this book Information Technology is a way of working. Here you will find ideas and suggestions about how the tools of Information Technology can help you to work more efficiently and effectively in all your subjects. On each page you are invited to pick up these tools and go to work with them.

The book has five chapters plus a glossary which explains the terms used in IT:

At the beginning of each chapter there is a table of 'IT ideas for each subject', along with a page introducing the relevant aspect of IT. Many of the ideas in the table are explained in greater detail in the pages which follow. Each relates to one or two particular subjects, such as Maths or Art, but this does not mean that the skill can only be used in that subject. For example, a page about working with computers or a video camera in History may also give you further ideas for doing similar things in RE, French, Geography or English.

When using IT, you will learn:

Some pages have boxes (like this one) which identify the IT skills you will be using

Whether you are investigating a problem in Science, trying out new ideas in Technology or working with graphs and charts in Maths, the important point is that *you* choose the way to work. If Information Technology helps you to work more effectively, use it. If another way of working is better, use that. But you can only decide when you know what IT is all about.

1 COMMUNICATING INFORMATION

IT IDEAS FOR EACH SUBJECT

English	◆ Reconstruct a poem on screen and present a new version for class discussion **see page 10**. ◇ Make a front page newspaper story based upon an incident in a novel or play.
Maths	◆ Chart and publish a survey of class opinions **see page 16**. ◇ Make a booklet with accompanying worksheets, which explain and illustrate probability theory.
Science	◆ Dramatize on video an important scientific discovery **see page 20**. ◇ Make an introductory guide to a branch of the animal kingdom.
Technology	◇ Mount a display of different computer-aided designs for birthday cards to establish consumer preferences. ◇ Design a menu for a special occasion.
Modern Languages	◆ Make a local trade directory for foreign visitors **see page 12**. ◇ Make a personal ID card.
Geography	◇ Make a video describing recent economic growth/decline in the area and its impact on the locality. ◇ Write a newspaper report about the effects of a volcanic eruption.
History	◆ Reproduce a historical document using appropriate fonts **see page 8**. ◆ Dramatize on video an important historical event **see page 20**.
Art	◆ Design a record sleeve **see page 18**. ◇ Mount an exhibition of class computer art work with a descriptive catalogue.
Music	◇ Compose a jingle to advertise a healthy eating product. ◇ Devise an entertainment which sets poetry to computer-generated music.
PE	◇ Make an information sheet of warm-up exercises for a specific activity. ◇ Design an activity schedule for an overweight child or adult.
RE/PSE	◇ Produce a feature article on a religious or moral issue after interviewing a cross-section of pupils in school. ◇ Make a video of worship in the community.
Economic & Industrial Understanding	◇ Design a questionnaire to identify pupil/parent preferences for different Christmas decorations, as part of a school-based business. ◇ Make a video of different advertising techniques which might be used to sell a product.
Careers	◇ Create an imaginary personal CV at the age of twenty, thirty and forty. ◇ Make an anti-sexist video for a discussion which dramatizes stereotypical attitudes towards career choice.
Health	◇ Produce a leaflet to publicize the benefits of using the local gym. ◇ Design a symbol appropriate to health and safety in a particular situation.
Citizenship	◆ Promote a point of view in a public debate **see page 14**. ◇ Raise awareness of the effects of vandalism on the community through a display of photographs and word-processed text.
Environmental Education	◆ Give a foyer display to promote the school and improve its appearance **see page 6**. ◇ Give a presentation using text, statistics and graphs, on an environmental problem.

Times of change

We are living through times of rapid change. Information Technology has transformed all our lives. In particular, it has changed the way we communicate information. We can both send and receive information in the form of words, pictures and sounds by using the astonishing power of the machines of the Information Technology revolution. Never before have we been able to communicate so much, so far, so quickly.

Businesses and industry no longer need to rely on the postal service to pass on information. They can send letters, reports, drawings, orders and plans by electronic mail or by a facsimile (fax) machine, using the telephone lines. These forms of communication are instant – and, in business, time is money.

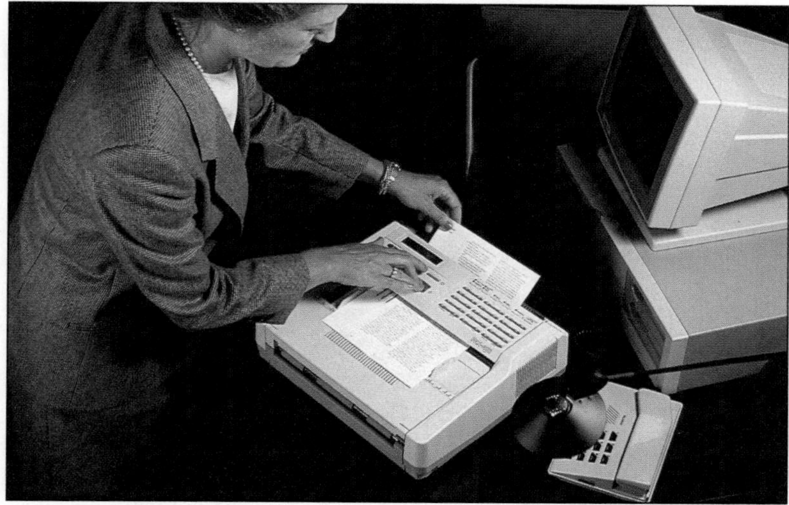

△ **Fig. 1.1 Fax machine**

△ **Fig. 1.2 Communications satellite**

The use of satellite communications has meant that we can see television reports and programmes coming to us live from distant parts of the world: a world-wide audience is now able to watch the international soccer matches as they take place, and the Live Aid concert at Wembley was transmitted all over the world.

Advanced telecommunications have enabled groups of people to hold conferences and to discuss important issues, even though they are in different countries. They do this through video link-ups (sometimes called videoconferencing) or teleconferencing.

Developments in communications also allow us to do much more from our own homes. Through the use of viewdata systems, for example, we can book holidays and do teleshopping. Some organizations encourage their employees to work from home, communicating with one another electronically, via a computer network.

In school, you will have tape recorders, video cameras and computers equipped with word-processing and desk-top publishing software. These will enable you to communicate your ideas to other people in words, pictures and sounds. At the same time, they will help you to present your work accurately and attractively.

△ **Fig. 1.3 Using a DTP package**

Putting the School *on*

The image which you present to other people is very important: how you appear communicates a good deal about you as a person. The same applies to your school.

Take a look round your school environment: what image does it communicate to someone coming in for the first time? Are the wall displays attractive? Do they show a visitor what is special about your school? Are the different parts of the school well signposted?

Perhaps you could improve your school environment by designing new, original wall displays. Using the tools of Information Technology, you can develop a more professional standard of presentation, conveying a positive image of your school.

△ **Fig. 1.4 Professional-looking signs**

△ **Fig. 1.5 Computer-generated material for display**

> When using IT, you will learn:
>
> *to integrate more than one form of information into a single presentation or report for a particular audience*

PRESENTATION IDEAS

Make notices for the entrance hall to help visitors find their way round the school. These might be just word-processed text, printed out in various sizes and colours.

You might like to communicate information in pictures by using appropriate images alongside the words. You could do this by photocopying illustrations, including fancy scrolls, frames and borders, or you could use clip art. If you have a scanner, you will be able to transfer your illustrations into your computer software. You could then enlarge or reduce the illustrations before positioning them alongside the words. Some computer software already has its own library of illustrations, which can be combined with your text.

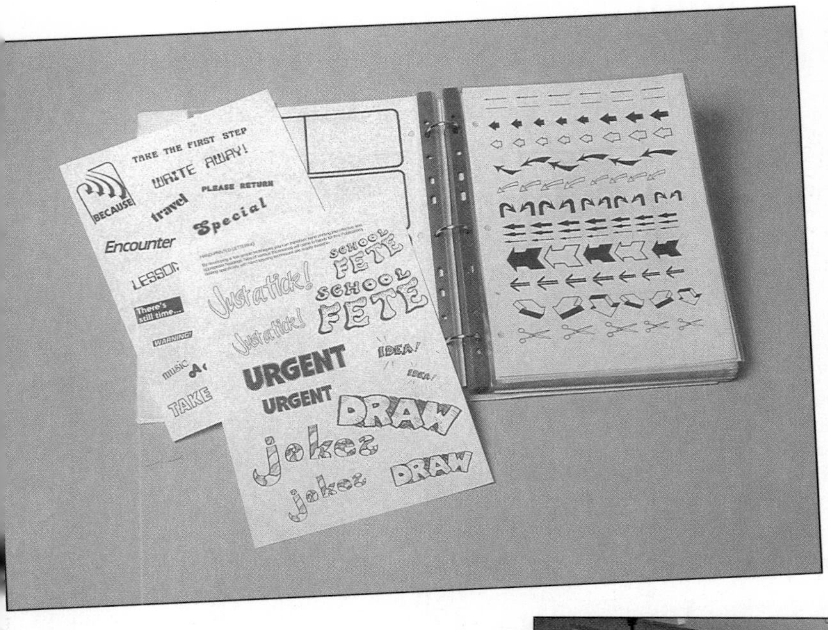

MOUNTING PHOTOGRAPHS

Show the school at work and at play by taking a selection of photographs of pupils in the classroom and playground. Mount the best photographs alongside a short word-processed explanation of what is happening.

If your school is proud of its sporting achievements, mount a display of photographs showing the different kinds of sporting activities which your school encourages. Your text might be put together after interviewing the pupils in the photographs. You could make further use of this material by including some of it in a school Sports Day programme.

◁ **Fig. 1.6 Pages of clip art ready to be scanned**

VIDEO IMAGES

When the school has a special event like a Maths–Industry Day or is playing host to a local sporting event, record what happens on video. Decide which frames on the video tape are worth putting on display. Using a video digitizer, you can then transform the images into screens which can be printed out or imported into your software.

△ **Fig. 1.7 Scanning an illustration into an Archimedes system**

△ **Fig. 1.8 An attractive welcome for the school visitor**

If any of your displays are made for permanent use you could keep them looking new by laminating them. Similarly, any display of images and text can be protected by perspex. In both cases, your presentation of your information will look professional, and project an attractive image of you and the school to visitors.

If you are particularly pleased with the impact of the IT work on the school environment, why not take a photograph for inclusion in the school brochure?

Neat forgeries

Using a word processor can make writing an easier and less frustrating activity. Whether you are collecting together information or writing to a friend, it's easy to delete words and insert others at the press of a button. Compare the speed and efficiency of this process with that of the medieval scribe in Fig. 1.9. He not only had to cross or scrape out any mistakes he made, he also had to write out each copy of his book by hand, since printing did not exist.

A word processor can also help you present your work in an attractive way. The final product will be pleasing to both you and your audience. Using a word processor can bring your work to life. Many word-processing programs have special fonts with old-fashioned scripts, as well as modern typefaces. If you are writing an eye-witness account of some aspect of life in the past, for example, you can choose a font which looks like the writing of someone living at that time.

△ **Fig. 1.9**

△ **Fig. 1.10 Holbein's Dance of Death**

When using IT, you will learn:

- *to select software for a task or application*
- *that IT can be used to do things which can also be done in other ways*

THE BLACK DEATH CHRONICLE

Imagine that you are living in the middle of the fourteenth century. A killer is at large, invisible and invincible. Its touch means pain, suffering and a slow, agonizing death. The Black Death has made itself at home in England.

Now imagine that you are a monk living through this catastrophe. Many of your friends in the monastery have met the same fate as the monk pictured in Fig. 1.10. You can only watch, as normal life falls apart, but unlike most men and women of the time you can read and write. You are, therefore, in a position to record what is happening all around you; you can do the job of the monastic chronicler.

MEDIEVAL MANUSCRIPTS

Whether you are working alone or in a group, your first ideas could be put into any word processor. After you have thought about them and discussed them further, you may want to alter and rearrange what you have typed. Whatever you write, if you choose a font which is appropriate to the fourteenth, rather than to the twentieth century, your work will look more authentic.

The plague killed Jew, Christian and Saracen alike: it carried off those who were sinful and those who lived virtuous lives. In many places hardly one fifth of the population were left alive. The whole world was filled with terror at the pestilence. So great an epidemic has never been seen nor heard of before this sorrowful time. For it is believed that even the waters of the flood which filled the world in the days of Noah did not carry off so many. In this year many monks of our monastery have perished.

Ora pro nobis

Compare the two examples of word-processed work. Which is more effective? Look at the students producing their medieval manuscript in Fig. 1.11. Could you do that?

When your text is printed out, it will be crisp, clean and new. What could you do in order to make it appear over six hundred years old and, therefore, more authentic?

◁ **Fig. 1.11**

The plague killed Jew, Christian and Saracen alike: it carried off those who were sinful and those who lived virtuous lives. In many places hardly one fifth of the population were left alive. The whole world was filled with terror at the pestilence. So great an epidemic has never been seen nor heard of before this sorrowful time. For it is believed that even the waters of the flood which filled the world in the days of Noah did not carry off so many. In this year many monks of our monastery have perished.

Ora pro nobis

Having fun with

A poem is made out of words, just as a wall is made out of bricks. Like any wall, a poem can be knocked down and then rebuilt. The word processor is a very useful piece of machinery for helping you to demolish a poem and then to put it back together. After the poem has been rebuilt to your satisfaction, you can ask yourself these questions: how is this different from the poem I started with and have any improvements been made?

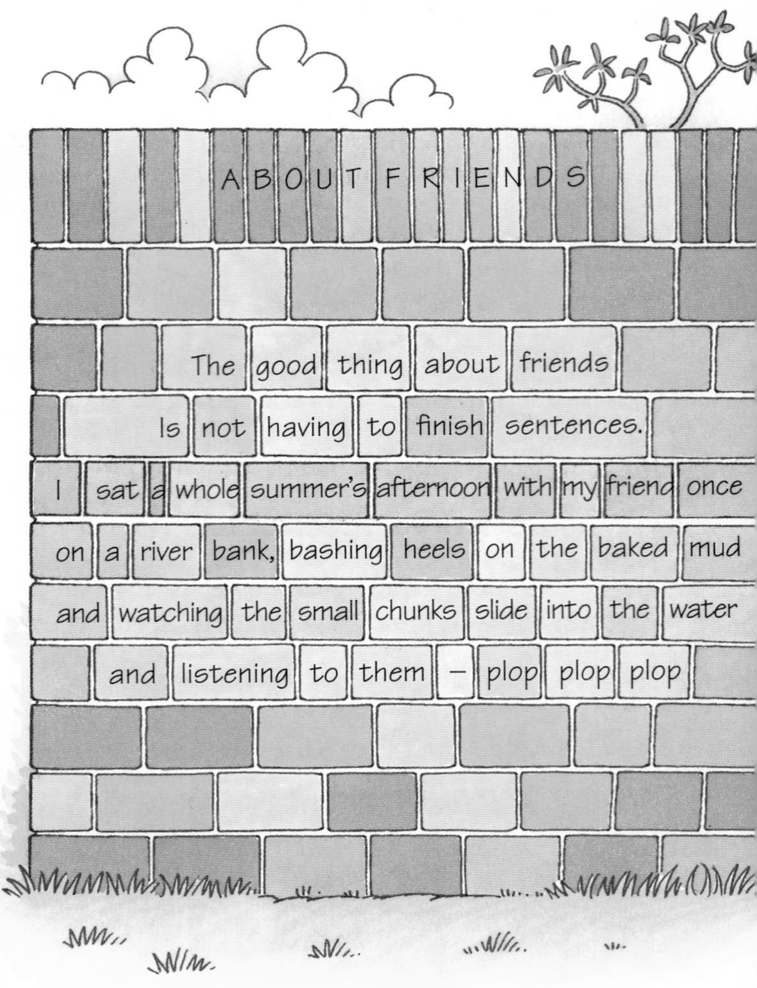

DEMOLITION

In small groups, choose a poem for knocking down. Perhaps it is a poem which looks at a subject which you are talking and writing about yourselves. Before going to the computer, plan the demolition of the poem first. Read the poem through and decide which the most important or interesting words are. You may choose to delete all the adjectives. For example,when a writer described a young girl in a telephone booth on a cold night 'huddled in her flimsy coat', he was relying a lot upon the words 'huddled' and 'flimsy'. He was building up a picture of coldness, which the words 'in her coat', on their own, would fail to do. You could decide to remove all the nouns. This would enable you to change the subject matter of the poem instead.

When you have decided upon the demolition plan, type the poem on to the screen with the most powerful words missing. Make sure that you leave spaces on the screen where the words used to be. Once you are satisfied with the demolition, print it out and distribute it to the other groups.

When using IT, you will learn:

to put existing information into a new format, taking account of the audience

RECONSTRUCTION

As the demolition workers, your group knows what the original poem looked like. The rest of the class does not. Now you can set the other groups in the class the task of rebuilding your poem. Print out your work for each group and ask them to think about what the missing words might be. Once the different groups have tried to reconstruct your poem, type their words into the computer and print out the new versions, as well as a complete version of the original poem.

EVALUATION

The class will end up with several new versions of your poem. Pin them up on the wall and examine each new construction. What changes have been made? Have some groups used the same material as the author in rebuilding the poem? Is the new material stronger than the original material? Ask someone from each group to explain how they made their decisions.

△ **Fig. 1.14**

POSTER POEMS

Find or create images which match up with the contents of your poems. Make a display of poster poems using all the new versions of the poem, as well as the original poem.

EURO LINKS

Fig. 1.15 Trade directories ▷

If your school has a foreign-language exchange arranged with a school in France or Germany, the children visiting your area for the first time face a difficult situation. They not only have to find their way around a strange place, but also have to communicate in a different language from their own.

Looking for something to do on a wet afternoon?

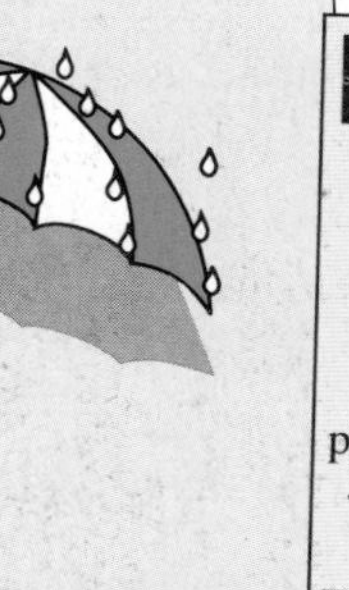

Visit Hull City Art Gallery
23 Highgate

ALL SORTS FOR ALL SPORTS

Including
Badminton – Squash – Roller Skating – Hard play area for 5-a-side Football – Synthetic pitch all year round – Indoor pole vaulting – Tennis – Hockey – Netball – Junior Gym Club – Children's Sessions – Dance Exercise – Aerobics

PETER PAINE SPORTS CENTRE
Rosebery Avenue, Boston
Tel: 3502

TRADE DIRECTORIES

In order to help your foreign visitors to get the most out of their visit, why not create a Trade Directory in French or German, using a desk-top publishing package?

Trade directories are booklets which give the reader useful information about the kinds of services which are to be found in the town and where they are situated. They are also a valuable way for local businesses and shops to advertise their services.

COLLECTING INFORMATION

First, have a look at a selection of trade directories to examine the different kinds of information which are found there and how this information is presented on the page. Since you are making a booklet for a particular group, you have to ask yourself what kind of information they would need. Clearly there are services in your area which they would not require, such as a plumber or a residential home for the elderly. On the other hand, the children visiting your area may want to know about supermarkets, banks and local places of interest.

Once you have decided which information you are going to include in your Trade Directory, you could divide the workload up so that different groups in the class are responsible for different categories of information. One group, for example, might be in charge of creating information pages about entertainment and leisure facilities. Another group might concentrate on supplying a list of gift shops in the area.

When using IT, you will learn:

to review and discuss your use of IT applications and consider related applications in the outside world and their impact on everyday life

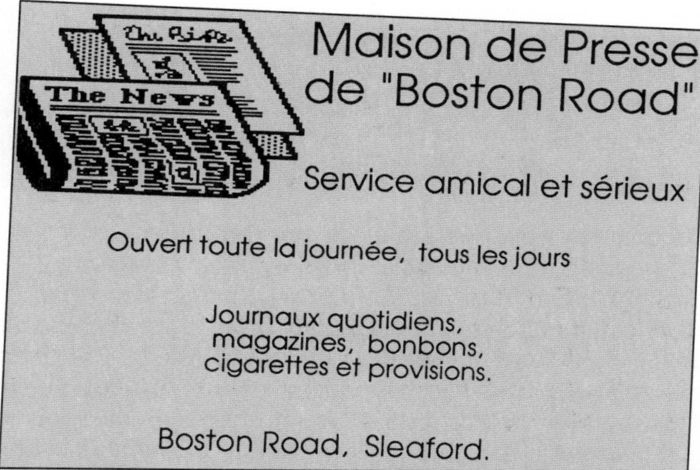

DESIGN DECISIONS

First, decide which language you are going to work in, then, before starting work on your pages, consider which desk-top publishing package is the most suitable for your work. Answer these questions to help you decide:

- Does it have a wide variety of fonts with which to present your information?
- Are you able to stretch, reduce and move text around?
- Does it have a choice of page formats?
- Can you easily integrate text with any appropriate graphics which you have chosen?

SPECTRUM HAIR

POUR LES GENS
AUX CHEVEUX
LONGS.

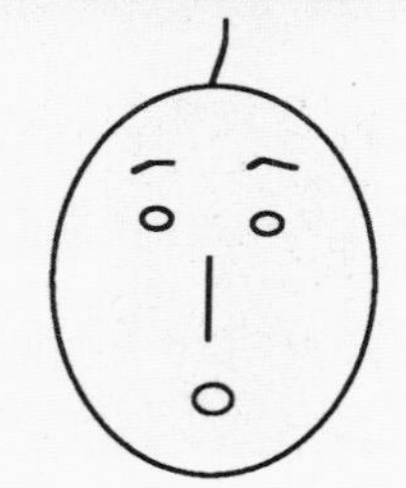

Handley Court Mews , SLEAFORD

TEL : (0529) 4135

You will also need to consider what kind of information is appropriate to each advertisement, as well as deciding upon the most effective graphics. You might also show what you are planning to the owners of the businesses in your own local Trade Directory. They may be able to offer their expertise in marketing and advertising to help you communicate your ideas clearly and concisely.

PRINTING AND DISTRIBUTING

Once you have created your pages, printed them out, and arranged them in booklet form you can send off copies to your French or German guests, perhaps as part of a school information pack.

MAKING YOUR CASE

Schools have changed in many ways during the last thirty years, notably in the way pupils have become more involved in the running of the school. More and more schools have School Council meetings in which the voice of the pupil is heard and taken seriously. But there are good and bad ways of presenting your point of view. The key to success is being well prepared so that you can present your point of view effectively, using all the resources which are available. One of the best resources which you have is Information Technology.

With a database to collect and sort information and a word processor for high quality presentation of your ideas, you will be able to make your point clearly and impressively.

Let us imagine that your class feels that the morning assembly needs livening up. The pupils would like to participate more fully in the actual assembly and in deciding its format. What might be the best way of pressing for the changes you want to see? A good start would be for the class to sit down and discuss how to involve as many people as possible.

△ **Fig. 1.16 School Council**

When using IT, you will learn:

to identify clearly the requirements and make correct use of IT equipment, software and techniques in making presentations and reports

PREPARE

To make a start, you might devise a questionnaire by producing it on a word processor, printing it out and distributing it to every pupil in the school. Alternatively, you might use a software database which allows you to create a questionnaire on screen. This kind of software also calculates the results of your survey. Whatever method is used, you clearly need to decide upon the kind of questions which are to be included in your survey, so that you can collect useful and precise information.

PRESENT

While gathering information from around the school you also need to prepare and plan how you are going to present your ideas and your findings from the questionnaire. The key to an effective presentation is to communicate your ideas clearly and simply, so that they are easily understood. To make out a case for changing the assembly you could use the computer to produce a document which puts together your ideas and the results of your survey.

Notice the differences between the computer-generated document and the handwritten page in Fig. 1.17. Which one is the more professional? Which would be more successful in communicating your views?

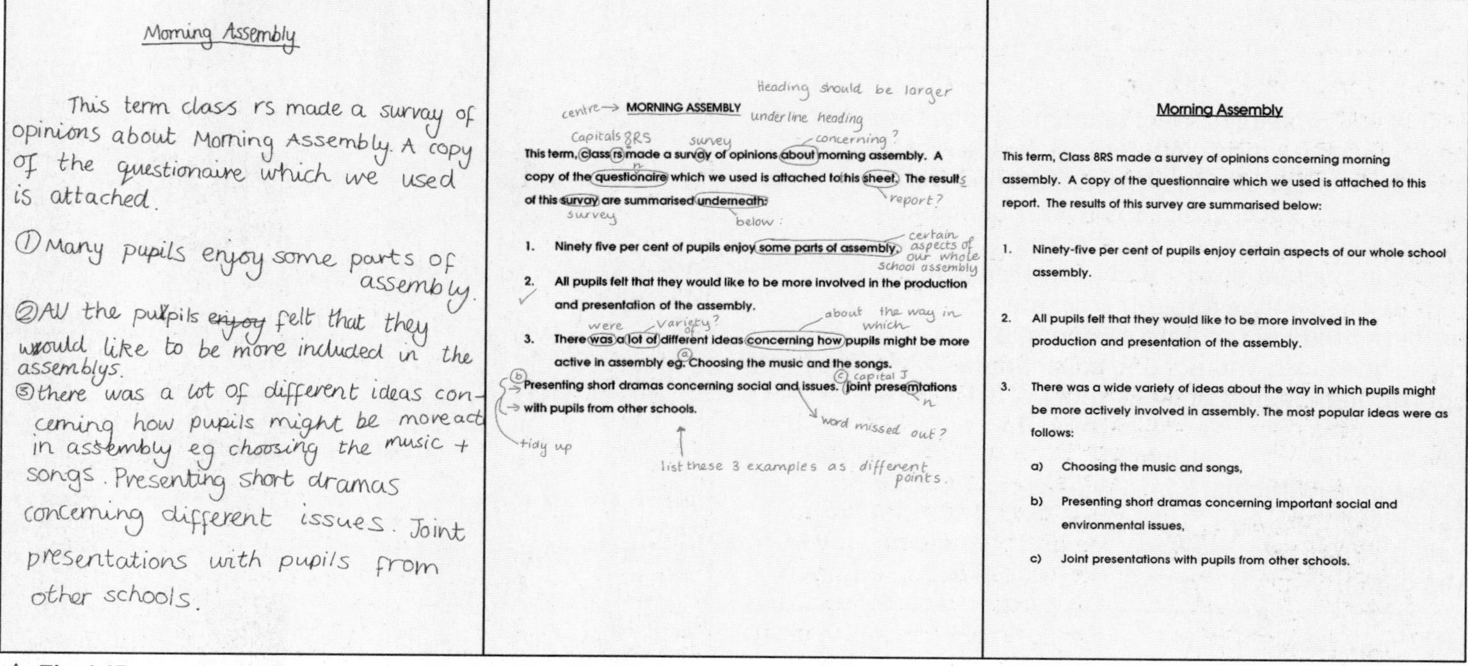

Morning Assembly

This term class rs made a survay of opinions about Morning Assembly. A copy of the questionaire which we used is attached.

① Many pupils enjoy some parts of assembly.

② All the pulpils ~~enjoy~~ felt that they would like to be more included in the assemblys.

③ there was a lot of different ideas concerning how pupils might be more act in assembly eg choosing the music + songs. Presenting short dramas concerning different issues. Joint presentations with pupils from other schools.

MORNING ASSEMBLY

This term, class rs made a survay of opinions about morning assembly. A copy of the questionaire which we used is attached to this sheet. The result of this survay are summarised underneath:

1. Ninety five per cent of pupils enjoy some parts of assembly.
2. All pupils felt that they would like to be more involved in the production and presentation of the assembly.
3. There was a lot of different ideas concerning how pupils might be more active in assembly eg. Choosing the music and the songs. Presenting short dramas concerning social and issues. joint presentations with pupils from other schools.

Morning Assembly

This term, Class 8RS made a survey of opinions concerning morning assembly. A copy of the questionnaire which we used is attached to this report. The results of this survey are summarised below:

1. Ninety-five per cent of pupils enjoy certain aspects of our whole school assembly.
2. All pupils felt that they would like to be more involved in the production and presentation of the assembly.
3. There was a wide variety of ideas about the way in which pupils might be more actively involved in assembly. The most popular ideas were as follows:
   a) Choosing the music and songs,
   b) Presenting short dramas concerning important social and environmental issues,
   c) Joint presentations with pupils from other schools.

△ **Fig. 1.17**

△ **Fig. 1.18 A lively assembly**

PARTICIPATE

Now that you have a document which looks good and represents the majority view of the pupils, what do you do with it? Perhaps the best idea might be to show it to your form teacher for discussion in tutorial time, so that those pupils who may not agree with your views, can, at least, consider your ideas and communicate *their* opinions. This discussion would be useful because it might give you fresh ideas to put into your document and improve it. Think of the advantages of having used a computer if that is the case. In the end, you will need to discuss your ideas and investigations with the headteacher, either in a small meeting or in a session of the School Council. Whenever you discuss an issue of school policy, the resources of Information Technology will help you to present your case and you will impress your audience by the professional way in which you have participated in the running of your school.

CHARTING the latest trends

If someone from another class asked you the following questions concerning the current likes and dislikes of your class, would you be able to answer them with any accuracy?

- What are your class's favourite television programmes?
- Which films have your class enjoyed most in the last month?
- Which are currently the most popular kinds of music in your class?

You would probably have a rough idea of all the answers, based on your conversations with the rest of the class and on your knowledge of what films and records are currently successful. However, being able to produce an accurate report of the class's tastes in popular music, film and television, requires more than a rough estimate. In order to produce accurate answers to these questions you need to collect data, sort through it, and present your findings in a clear way. You could do all this by hand, but it would be far more difficult, especially the sorting of the data.

NAME	Thomas Moyes
FORM	7x
DATE	9th March 1993
QUESTION	
What type of music do you like the most?	Reggae, Heavy Metal, Ska, Blues, Soul, Rap, Rock, Other.
Which soap do you watch most often during the week?	Home and Away, Neighbours, Eldorado, Coronation Street, EastEnders, None.
What kind of films do you prefer?	Comedy, Thriller, Cartoons Adventure, Science Fiction, Horror, Other.

△ **Fig. 1.19 Data capture sheet**

When using IT, you will learn:

to use IT for investigations requiring analysis of data

to collect and organize information for entry into a database

CREATING A QUESTIONNAIRE

First, you need to design a simple questionnaire, using boxes and columns. You could do this by hand, but creating it on a computer would have many advantages: it would be easier to make alterations, for example, as well as more convenient to store and use again in the future. Whichever way of working you choose, remember to make the sheet as simple as possible, so that each question is easily understood and answered.

If you decide to use a computer to produce your questionnaire, you could create it using a word-processing package, as in Fig. 1.19. Alternatively, your school's software library may have a program which enables you to produce a computer-generated questionnaire on the screen, as in Fig. 1.20.

COLLECTING DATA

When you have produced all your questionnaire sheets, give them out to members of your class to fill in. Then, collect the forms and decide how you are going to present the data to the rest of the class. You could go through the questionnaire, section by section, counting up the number of people who have similar answers. This might be followed by drawing a bar graph or a pie chart to illustrate your data.

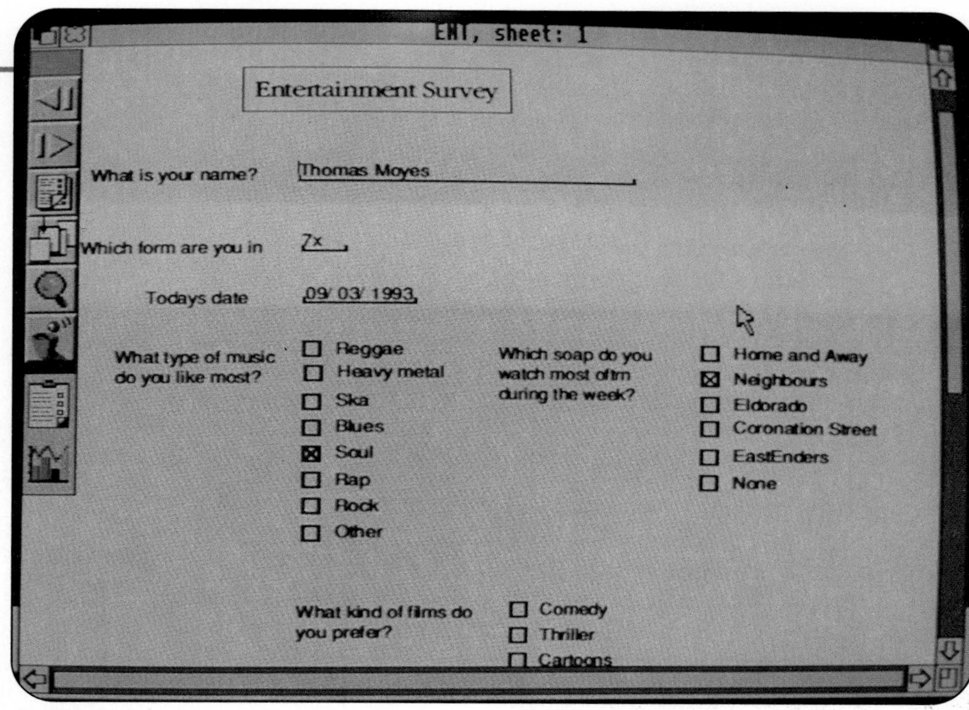

△ **Fig. 1.20**

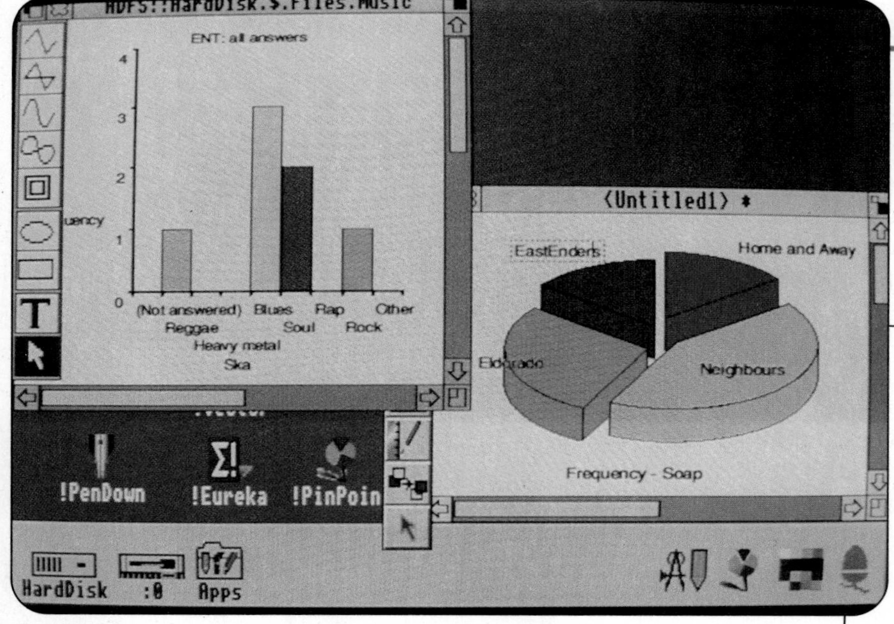

△ **Fig. 1.21**

PRESENTING RESULTS

On the other hand, you could use the database and spreadsheet programs in your software library. These can analyse the data fed into them and present the results in the form of graphs and charts (as in Fig. 1.21). Using this kind of software will save you a lot of time and will also enable you to present the data more precisely.

To accompany your charts or graphs, you could word process an explanation of the survey and interpret the results for the reader (as in Fig. 1.22). Both your text and your graphs or charts could be displayed in your classroom, or made into a book recording the class's tastes that term.

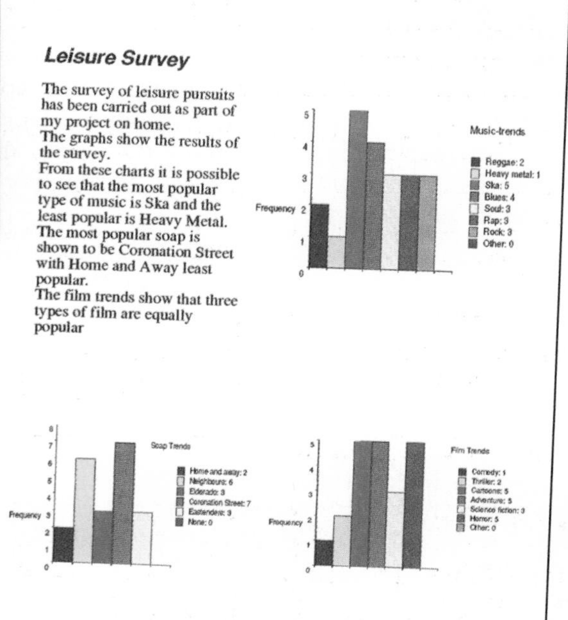

Leisure Survey

The survey of leisure pursuits has been carried out as part of my project on home.
The graphs show the results of the survey.
From these charts it is possible to see that the most popular type of music is Ska and the least popular is Heavy Metal.
The most popular soap is shown to be Coronation Street with Home and Away least popular.
The film trends show that three types of film are equally popular

Fig. 1.22 ▷

The word-processing facilities of the computer are ideal for drafting and redrafting your poems and essays. You can alter, add and take away sections of text or save different versions of your work as text files. This is also true of the graphics programs which might be used in a design project, such as making a record cover. The facilities of your graphics programs will allow you to experiment with colour and shape, as well as to consider your work in various different versions.

If your parents or grandparents have a record collection dating back to when they were young, compare it with your own collection of tapes and records. What differences do you see? Many of the singers or groups you will never have heard of before. If the singles are still in their original covers, you will notice that these also differ greatly from the record sleeves of today.

DESIGN FOR A SONG

Have a look at the singles in Fig. 1.23. In the 1950s and 1960s each record company had a standard paper cover which they used for all their singles, like the one at the top. The cover tells us the name of the record company and very little else. Now take a look at the other two covers: each one has been individually designed for a particular song. Considerable time and effort has gone into creating these special designs – the designers have chosen an image and a font which they thought would be striking and appropriate to the music. In short, the covers are helping to sell the records by creating an exciting visual impact, an effect which the plain paper sleeve does not have.

CLASS FAVOURITES

Get your classmates to bring in a selection of covers from their own music collections and compare the ways in which each designer has tried to make a visual impact upon the buyer. Which ones are the class favourites? Which ones do you feel are not very successful in attracting the buyer and why not?

Unfortunately, unless we know the designer personally or have the opportunity for an interview, we will never know how ideas develop in his or her imagination. But we can be sure that there are many stages between starting the design and the production of the final product, in which ideas are considered, tried out and rejected.

△ **Fig. 1.23**

When using IT, you will learn:

to organize, develop and present ideas in a variety of forms by using software packages

to find and present stored information

COVER VERSIONS

Imagine that you have been asked to design a record cover for your favourite group's latest single. How would you go about it? You need to decide first upon the materials which will be necessary. You might use pen or coloured pencils to work out your ideas on paper. This is certainly one approach to the task.

On the other hand, you might choose to use a piece of software to help you design the record sleeve. What advantages would there be in doing it this way?

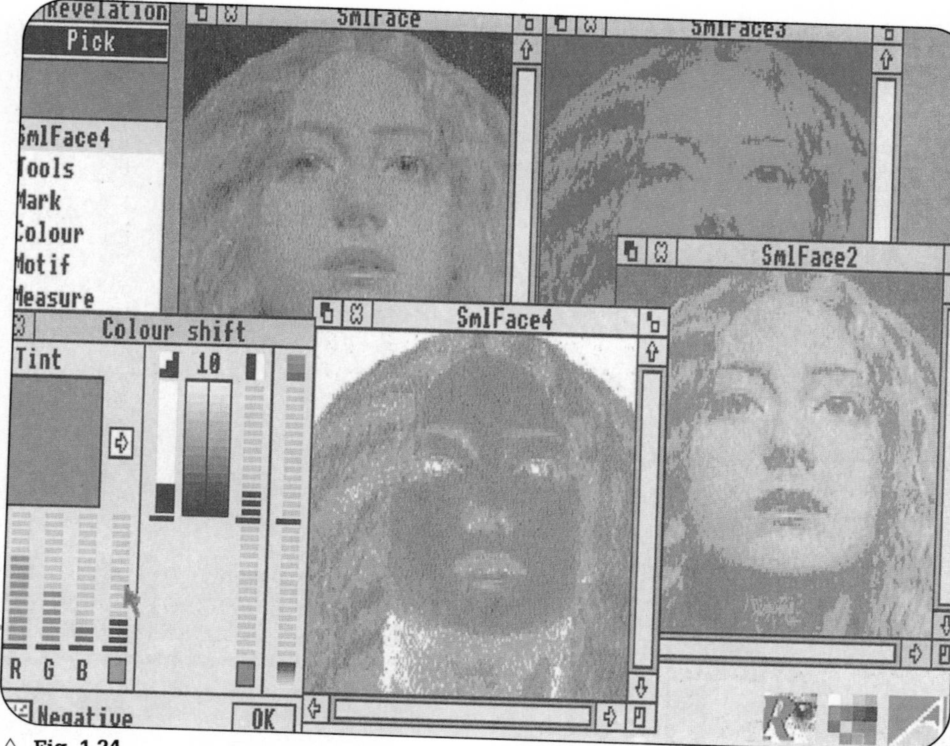

△ **Fig. 1.24**

ALTERED IMAGES

Think about the number of times we change our minds when designing a picture, as well as the alterations we make after our friends have looked at our work and made their comments. Designing on screen means we can make corrections and additions at any stage, whereas if traditional painters made mistakes they would have to start all over again.

Also, think of the convenience of having several versions of an image or different text design on screen at the same time, as in the program in Fig. 1.24.

You will be aiming to produce a cover which encourages the record buyer to part with money. But it might be very interesting to let the rest of your class into the secret workings of your imagination by keeping a copy of each stage of your design. Having chosen to use the computer, all you have to do is store each stage of the design on a separate file in the program you are using. You might also keep a set of notes on the kinds of problems you were trying to solve and what you were trying to achieve at each stage of your work. This way you won't forget any of the details of the story of your design.

STAGE SHOW

When you have decided upon a final design for your record sleeve, you could mount a small exhibition of your work, by displaying your designs in the order in which you created them for your class to view. Don't forget to include the images, fonts and colours which you rejected. After you have mounted your work as it progressed, you might use the notes which were made during the course of the work to make a tape-recorded commentary on each stage of your design. This would help your audience to understand what you have produced and, perhaps more importantly, why you produced exactly what you did.

magic MOMENTS CAPTURED

Before the invention of the camera, it was impossible to capture a picture of the exact moment that something happened. Writers and artists might try later to reproduce those moments and episodes in words and paint, but to record them as they happened was not possible until technology helped us out.

What a pity that the video camera wasn't around to record the most extraordinary and exciting moments of the past. What episodes in the past would you have wanted to record?

- The execution of Charles I?
- The Great Fire of London in 1666?
- The opening of the Stockton–Darlington Railway?

△ **Fig. 1.25 Great Fire of London**

△ **Fig. 1.26 Execution of Charles I**

When using IT, you will learn:

to work together to prepare and present information using Information Technology

HISTORICAL REPLAY

There are, sadly, no video recordings of these past events. What you can do, however, if there is a video camera available, is to dramatize those great moments of the past yourselves and record them as if they were happenening for the first time.

Let's take as an example, the shock of a new idea and how people react to it. We all have ideas, but there are some new ideas which are shocking and frightening. These ideas are alarming because they seem to say that so many old, accepted ideas are wrong.

Charles Darwin was a nineteenth-century scientist who had some original ideas. He believed that humans evolved from the apes. This theory was so different that he kept it from other people for fifteen years. He thought that his ideas would shock other people, and that they would react with insults and abuse. He was right. After the publication of his book, *The Origin of Species*, in 1859, cartoons appeared showing Darwin as a monkey (as in Fig. 1.28) and jokes were cracked about men having apes for grandfathers.

◁ **Fig. 1.27 First journey of Stephenson's Rocket**

TELEVISION SENSATION

If the video camera had been around in 1859, Darwin and his book would have been a television sensation, but instead people found out about the new ideas from the newspaper, by borrowing library books or by going to public lectures on the subject of Evolution. But with the help of the school video camera, good planning and some imagination, you can capture on tape what the shock of Darwin's ideas might have been like.

The Research Team

Before you can decide what the people in your film are going to say, members of your group need to be appointed as Programme Researchers. The task is to find out what Darwin said, who was alarmed by his ideas and what they thought instead. So once you have appointed your Research Team just point them towards the Resource Centre.

The Presenters

The rest of the group need to discuss the best way of presenting the programme. Will it be set in the studio with someone interviewing Darwin and his enemies? Or will Darwin be facing a studio audience wanting to know about his ideas? Would you prefer to conduct interviews out on the street, asking people for their opinions? Have a look at real television programmes, to see how the professionals tackle similar problems.

Fig. 1.28

The Scriptwriters

When the Research Team returns and you have discussed the presentation, the whole group can write the script. First, decide at whom the programme will be aimed: another group in your class or children much younger than you? The script will be based on the material collected by your researchers, but you will have to use your imagination too. You might also think about the kind of music to be used during selected parts of the programme.

Shooting Schedule

The final task is for the group to agree upon a shooting schedule. This is a list of where the different scenes will be shot, what each scene will contain and when the shooting will take place. Perhaps this could be done on a word processor by one of the group and a copy given to each member.

Choose your actors, find some costumes, prepare the video camera, then you will be ready for ACTION.

Fig. 1.29

2 HANDLING INFORMATION

IT IDEAS FOR EACH SUBJECT

Subject	Ideas
English	◆ Create and update a database of personal reading **see page 36**. ◇ Collect information for a talk on a current issue using a newspaper on CD-ROM.
Maths	◇ Build up a class database of personal statistics and use it to test your theories on correlation. ◇ Create a spreadsheet to convert sterling into other European currencies.
Science	◆ Use a database to identify and classify species **see page 28**. ◇ Set up a spreadsheet to record and analyse experimental data.
Technology	◆ Use textual and graphic information to make different kinds of badges **see page 32**. ◇ Create a spreadsheet to analyse food prices in the locality.
Modern Languages	◇ Make a database in French/German as part of a computer dating agency simulation. ◇ Make a video recording of a choral reading of a French/German poem to improve presentation and pronunciation.
Geography	◇ Enter weather data into a database as part of a study of local climate. ◇ Collect and analyse data on patterns of household shopping to investigate distances travelled.
History	◆ Retrieve information from electronically stored manuscripts of historical documents **see page 40**. ◇ Use a database or spreadsheet to order and present census information.
Art	◇ Capture and store digitized images to use for preliminary sketches. ◇ Create a database of local artists.
Music	◆ Experiment with electronically generated sound to produce atmospheric effects **see page 24**. ◆ Edit and play back existing tune files **see page 24**.
PE	◆ Record personal performance on a spreadsheet to chart progress of a fitness programme **see page 30**. ◇ Use a video camera to improve techniques.
RE/PSE	◆ Retrieve information on religious festivals from encyclopaedias on CD-ROM **see page 40**. ◇ Make a database of local places of worship.
Economic & Industrial Understanding	◆ Chart and graph exchange rates on a spreadsheet to examine currency fluctuations **see page 26**. ◇ Collaborate in producing a word-processed script, using text and statistics, as part of a simulated enquiry into safety standards in a Victorian factory.
Careers	◆ Use on-line databases to find information on a particular career **see page 40**. ◇ Video and edit an interview with a local employer.
Health	◇ Collect video clips of advertisements for class discussion on gender stereotyping. ◆ Video children at a local playgroup to provide discussion material about child development **see page 34**.
Citizenship	◇ Search on-line databases for the names and addresses of caring agencies in preparation for a project on old age. ◆ Create datafiles of information to support a simulation involving ethical decision-making **see page 38**.
Environmental Education	◇ Use a database or a spreadsheet to record, analyse and graph the contents of the school dustbins as a starting point for discussing recycling and waste disposal. ◇ Devise a questionnaire to investigate local people's experience of noise pollution.

We are all information handlers

Even the simplest tasks we do involve the handling of information. Take, for example, crossing the road. You might think that such an ordinary activity as getting from one side of the road to the other would not require any information. But to cross a road you need to use a considerable amount. This information comes from what you have learnt from previous experiences and from what you see as you approach the road. In the split second between arriving at the kerb and deciding to cross the road, you will have handled the following basic pieces of information:

- Roads are used by vehicles.
- These vehicles are moving in two directions.
- Each vehicle is a certain distance away and is travelling at a certain speed.
- When vehicles collide with people the result is painful and sometimes fatal.
- It is crucial to look to the right and to the left in order to check that nothing is coming.
- If the road is clear in both directions, it is safe to cross.

Your senses of sight and hearing collect the evidence in front of you, then your brain processes this information and enables you to decide whether or not it is safe to cross the road.

Your mind is a wonderful piece of machinery for assimilating information, whether it is in the form of words, numbers, pictures or sounds.

MORE POWERFUL THAN THE MIND?

Computers are powerful information-handling tools too. In some ways they are more powerful than the human mind. They can retain more information and can sort through that information very quickly indeed.

For example, it would be impossible for one person to remember the name of every person living in this country. They would all have to be written down on pieces of paper. It would be doubly impossible to know their names *and* their dates of birth. Those, too, would have to be written down on pieces of paper, next to the appropriate name. The names would best be listed in alphabetical order, probably by surname. But imagine that you were trying to find out the names of all the people with the same first name *and* the same date of birth as you. You would have to check around 57 million names, one by one! Very slow and tedious! But because a computer can hold and process vast quantities of information very quickly, it could complete the search in a few seconds.

In only a short time, the tools of Information Technology have become part of everyday life, storing information in their large memories, sorting through it at astonishing speeds and retrieving answers in response to our demands. These labour-saving devices are now found in every area of our lives: in our homes, in shops and offices, and in our schools.

△ **Fig. 2.1 Handling information in the home …**

△ **Fig. 2.2 … in the street …**

△ **Fig. 2.3 … in school**

DIY MUSIC

You don't have to be an expert to make music. It has always been possible for everyone to have a go, but today it's easier than ever to succeed. You can now make real music using the school computer without knowing how to play a musical instrument or how to read music.

EXPERIMENTING WITH SOUNDS

With some software, all you have to do is press a key and sample the different sounds that are there for you to use. Other types of software use pictures on the screen to represent notes. When you are familiar with the different tunes you can then do more adventurous things such as combining the tunes together in different ways. Once you have done this, you might like to play around with your musical creation by altering the pitch and rhythm to see what kind of effects you can produce.

Other software has tune files for you to use which are by well-known musicians such as the Pet Shop Boys or Scott Joplin, as well as excerpts from famous composers such as Bach and Handel. The software enables you to experiment with its tune files by altering and rearranging them.

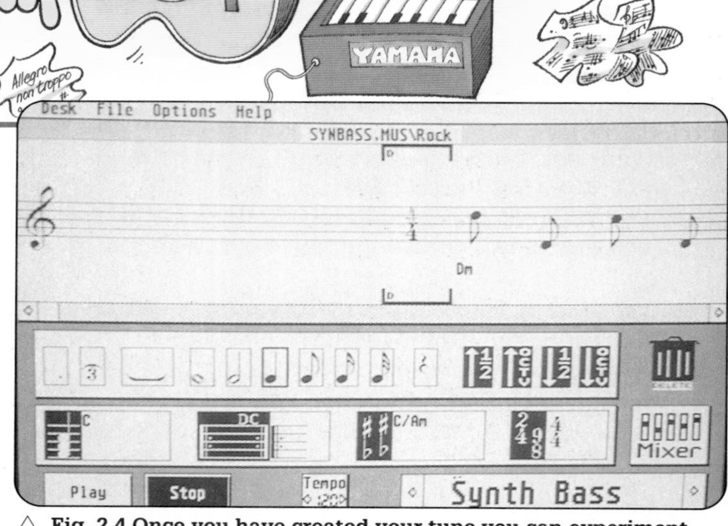

△ **Fig. 2.4 Once you have created your tune you can experiment with tempo and pitch.**

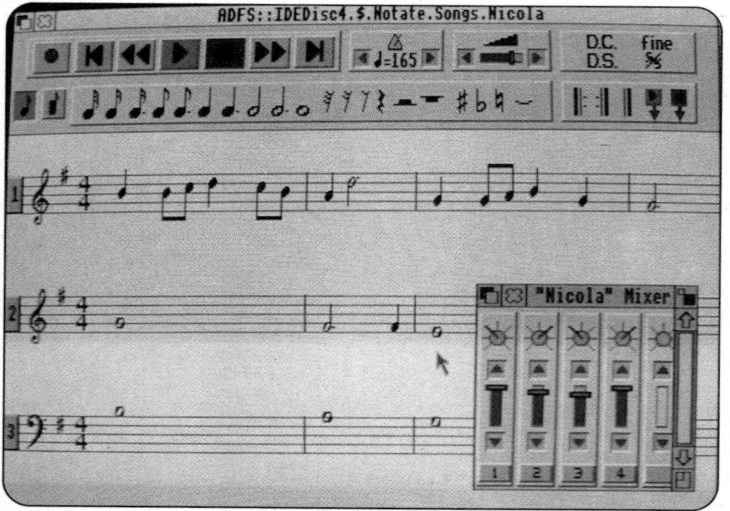

△ **Fig. 2.5 This program has pre-recorded tune files which you can retrieve and rearrange.**

When using IT, you will learn:

to identify clearly the requirements, and make correct use of information technology equipment, software and techniques, in making presentations

CREATING SOUNDS

If you create new sounds which you like, the software will allow you to save your work as a new tune file, just as a word processor enables you to keep your work on file so that you can come back to it another day.

If you have an electronic keyboard you will also be able to create and save your own music, either using the computer and a MIDI interface or by using a facility in the keyboard alone.

It's fun creating your own music from pictures on a computer screen, and you can also use these musical skills for a variety of different purposes. You might use the facilities of the software or the keyboard to create exciting atmospheric effects: music to go with the reading of a poem, or the opening music for your school play, for example.

Fig. 2.6 ▷

FILM SOUNDTRACKS

You could try creating the atmospheric sounds which are often used at the beginning of a film to get the viewer into the right frame of mind. What sort of music would go with these opening scenes?

- Waves crashing on the shore
- A ruined church surrounded in mist
- A spaceship floating through the Galaxy

First, get your teacher to record the opening music from a variety of different kinds of films; or you can listen to a sampler record of sound effects, if you have one in your record library. These will show you how the professionals have gone about making different kinds of atmospheric music and will perhaps give you ideas.

△ **Fig. 2.7**

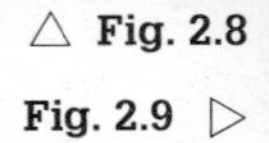

△ **Fig. 2.8**

Fig. 2.9 ▷

COMPUTER COMPOSERS

Once you have composed your own sequence of music using the computer software, the electronic keyboard or a combination of both, you might try some further experiments. For example, tape your music and then make a second track containing the voices of your friends producing different sound effects. When these two are complete, play them together and record them on to a master tape, so that you have an interesting combination of human voices and music, perhaps for the opening of a horror film. When you are satisfied that you have got the right combination of sounds, you could make a set of director's notes to go with your opening music, explaining what the audience might see while the music is playing, then play the final tape over the school's stereo system.

Getting value *for* MON£Y

A spreadsheet is a useful program for handling large amounts of data. It can store data, and helps you to make calculations based on this collected information. It can also produce graphs based on the data.

The sort of calculations which you might be interested in, for instance, could be how far your pocket money would stretch on a foreign holiday.

△ **Fig. 2.11 There are machines for exchanging one currency for another.**

Most people like to take foreign currency with them when they go on holiday. If you wanted to do this, your parents would have to exchange your pocket money before you went, either at a bank or a travel agent. The amount of foreign money which you would get for your English money would depend upon the Tourist Exchange Rate for that day. Clearly, if you are to get the best value for your money, choosing the right day on which to exchange your cash is important, since the exchange rate fluctuates constantly.

Your family might have decided, for example, to exchange £100 into francs three days before going to France. If the exchange rate on that day were 7.12 francs to one pound sterling, your total number of francs would be 712.

However, if your family decided to get the money changed on a different day, they might end up either with more francs if the Tourist Exchange Rate were higher than 7.12, or fewer, if the rate were lower.

WHAT'S THE DIFFERENCE?

In Fig.2.12. you will see the exchange rates for four days in August entered into a spreadsheet. Clearly, the best day for getting money exchanged was 4th August and the worst day was 1st August. The difference was 19 francs for the £100. This is not a very big difference – it would have been the cost of just six French bags of crisps!

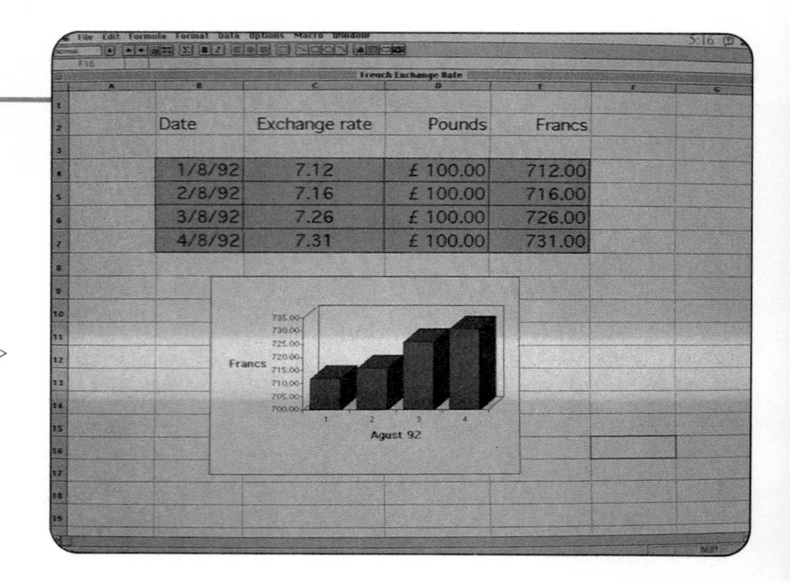

French Exchange Rate

Date	Exchange rate	Pounds	Francs
1/8/92	7.12	£ 100.00	712.00
2/8/92	7.16	£ 100.00	716.00
3/8/92	7.26	£ 100.00	726.00
4/8/92	7.31	£ 100.00	731.00

Fig. 2.12 Currency data on a spreadsheet ▷

When using IT, you will learn:

to organize, develop and present ideas in a variety of forms by using software packages

BIG MONEY

If you were running a business and you were dealing in hundreds of thousands (or even millions) of pounds, the difference between doing foreign business on 1st August and on 4th August would be crucial. It could make all the difference between profit and loss. Businesses, of course, do not change their money at travel agents. What they get for their pounds depends on the Business Exchange Rate, which can rise or fall in a matter of hours. Being able to analyse and predict the changes in the Business Exchange Rate would, therefore, be a very important skill indeed.

RECORDING AND GRAPHING

Using a hand-held calculator or by setting up the spreadsheet in Fig. 2.14, try working out the cost of exchanging half a million pounds on 1st August rather than on 4th August. Was the difference more than six bags of crisps?

Using the data recording and graphing facilities of your spreadsheet program, you could study currency fluctuations for yourself. You might do this over a period of a couple of weeks or over a much longer period of a few months. You could set up a spreadsheet which records information about one currency, or perhaps you would prefer to analyse the exchange rate for several currencies.

△ Fig. 2.13 International Financial Exchange

COLLECTING DATA

Once you have set up the labels on your spreadsheet you will have to collect your data. To find the exchange rate for the dates labelled in your spreadsheet, you could use various sources of information:

- Teletext
- Your Local Bank
- Newspapers
- On-line Databases

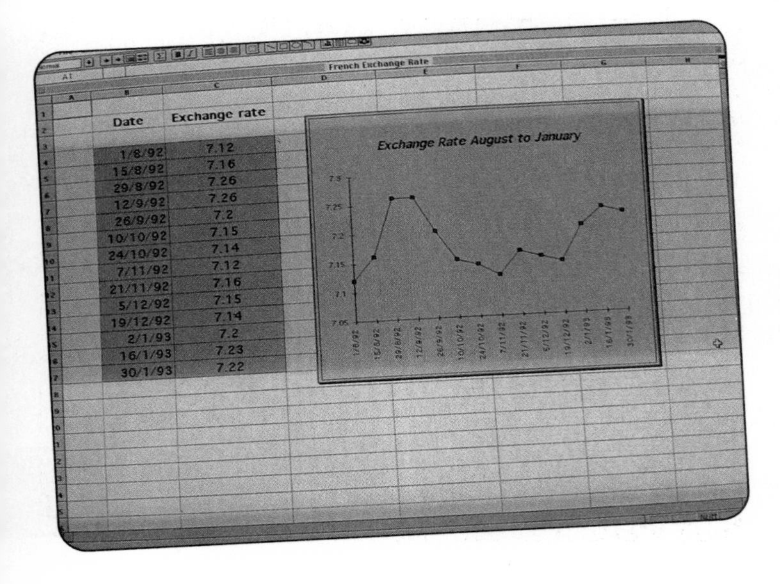

Date	Exchange rate
1/8/92	7.12
15/8/92	7.16
29/8/92	7.26
12/9/92	7.26
26/9/92	7.2
10/10/92	7.15
24/10/92	7.14
7/11/92	7.12
21/11/92	7.16
5/12/92	7.15
19/12/92	7.14
2/1/93	7.2
16/1/93	7.23
30/1/93	7.22

Once you have collected the data and entered it into your spreadsheet, you can convert this information into graph form, in order to examine the trends over a period of time. How much change was there in the exchange rate for your chosen currency? If you charted the fortunes of several currencies, which currency was the most stable and which one showed the greatest variation?

◁ Fig. 2.14 Currency fluctuations over a six month period

Seek and you will find – quickly

When you are doing project work – whatever the subject – managing your time is important. Information Technology can help you work more quickly and efficiently. If your project involves a large number of calculations, you could carefully work them out on paper. But using a calculator or a spreadsheet would save you time. If you have to sort through large amounts of information – in a science project, for example – you could save a lot of time by using a database.

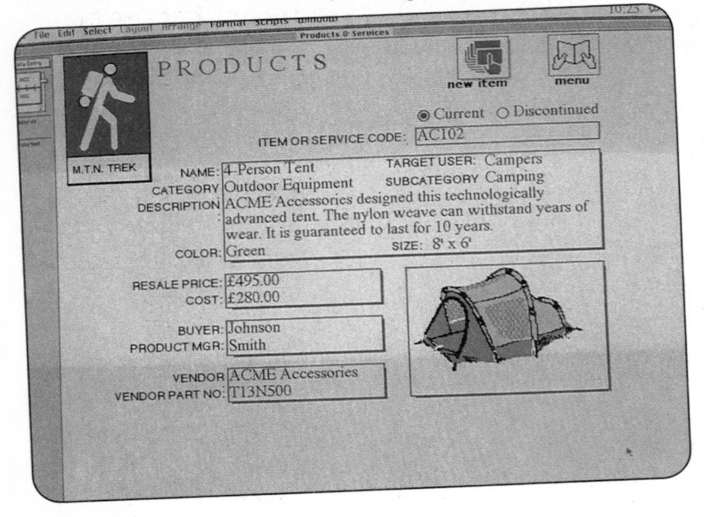

◁ Fig. 2.15

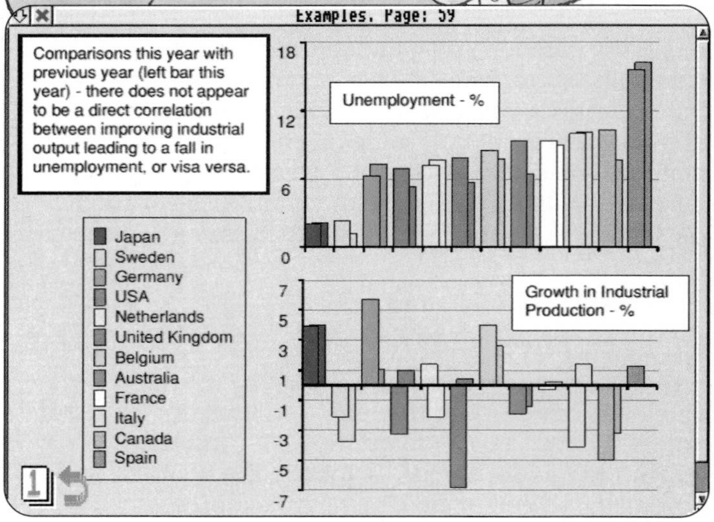

△ Fig 2.16

A database consists of a carefully organized collection of information stored on a computer as a datafile. A database program allows you to see the information you need (by searching the datafile), to edit, and to add new information. Software companies have produced datafiles on a wide variety of subjects (see Figs 2.15–2.17). Have a look in your school's software library to see what datafiles are available. By knowing what you have in school you will be able to plan your work better.

△ Fig 2.17

When using IT, you will learn:

to use search methods to obtain accurate and relevant information from a database

IDENTITY PARADE

In a science lesson you may have to investigate the different habitats that are found in your school grounds. Whatever habitats you choose (whether it is the soil, leaf litter, under stones or on trees) you will find many different creatures.

To identify the creatures you observe, you will first need to record details of their physical appearance and, if possible, make a sketch of them. Then, using this information, you could look through relevant books to identify the creatures. Alternatively, you could use an appropriate datafile (as in Fig. 2.19) to help you identify the creatures more quickly.

Fig. 2.18 ▷

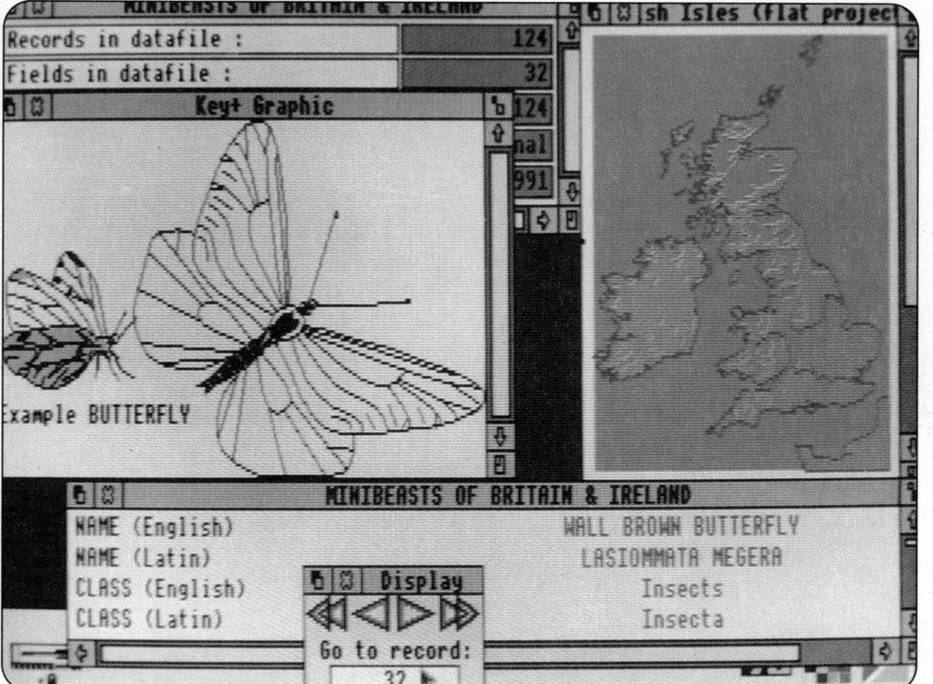

Your datafile might also provide you with pictures of the creatures, which you could compare with your sketches. These pictures could then be printed out and labelled according to your own observations.

To extend your work, you could use the datafile to find information about other creatures that live in the habitat you observed, to find out if they live in different habitats.

◁ **Fig. 2.19**

CLASSROOM CREATURES

All this information could be found by looking through books. But the computer is able to sort out information more quickly, and can therefore save you time.

As a follow-up to your investigation of the various habitats of creatures, you could set up a temporary home for them in the classroom. This would enable you to study their behaviour more closely and to collect further information about them. You could use a datafile to find out the right kind of living conditions for these creatures. For example, do orb-web spiders prefer damp or dry conditions? What do woodlice eat? What kind of soil best suits the wolf-spider? Do centipedes need to be in a warm environment?

◁ **Fig. 2.20**

FITNESS *for all*

Have you ever thought about using IT as part of your keep-fit programme? Exercise, like healthy eating, needs to be done regularly and with clear aims in mind, so it's a good idea to monitor your progress so that you are able to see what you have achieved. This will help you to work out whether or not your personal fitness programme is working and also encourage you to persevere with your exercise routine.

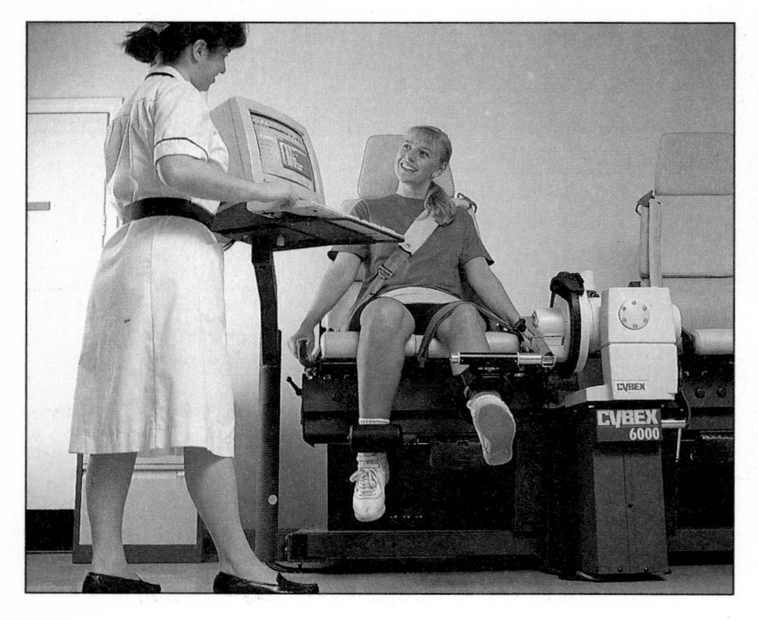

With a spreadsheet you can see at a glance what you have achieved in one activity over a set time. If you are doing a combination of activities it will also help you to see the progress of one activity in relation to another, so that comparisons can be made.

◁ **Fig. 2.21 Monitoring the progress of physiotherapy**

SETTING UP A SPREADSHEET

First, get the advice of your PE teacher or a qualified instructor, especially if you are using apparatus of any kind. Once you have agreed upon a set of aims and how you are going to fulfil those aims, you will be ready to set up your spreadsheet. You will need to enter appropriate labels relating to your activities and to the timescale in which you are working. Once the spreadsheet is set up, your data will accumulate over a period of time, showing how your fitness programme is progressing.

The spreadsheet in Fig.2.22 shows just one example of data from a general fitness programme. The data entered into the spreadsheet records progress in swimming, jogging and various activities in the multi-gym.

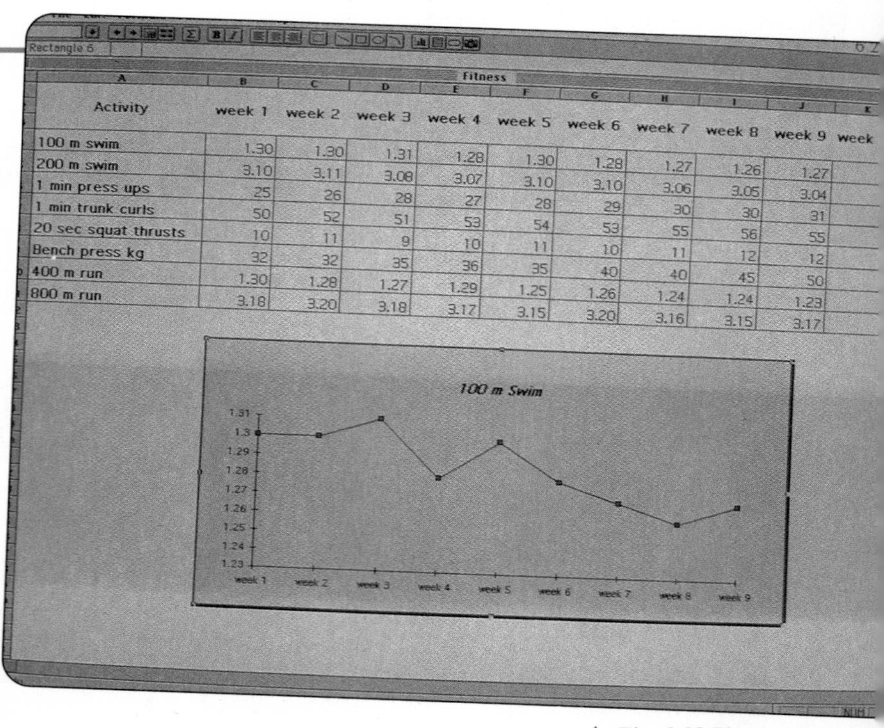

Fitness

Activity	week 1	week 2	week 3	week 4	week 5	week 6	week 7	week 8	week 9	week
100 m swim	1.30	1.30	1.31	1.28	1.30	1.28	1.27	1.26	1.27	
200 m swim	3.10	3.11	3.08	3.07	3.10	3.10	3.06	3.05	3.04	
1 min press ups	25	26	28	27	28	29	30	30	31	
1 min trunk curls	50	52	51	53	54	53	55	56	55	
20 sec squat thrusts	10	11	9	10	11	10	11	12	12	
Bench press kg	32	32	35	36	35	40	40	45	50	
400 m run	1.30	1.28	1.27	1.29	1.25	1.26	1.24	1.24	1.23	
800 m run	3.18	3.20	3.18	3.17	3.15	3.20	3.16	3.15	3.17	

△ **Fig. 2.22 Fitness data**

When using IT, you will learn:

that computers are used to store personal information

to use software packages confidently and well

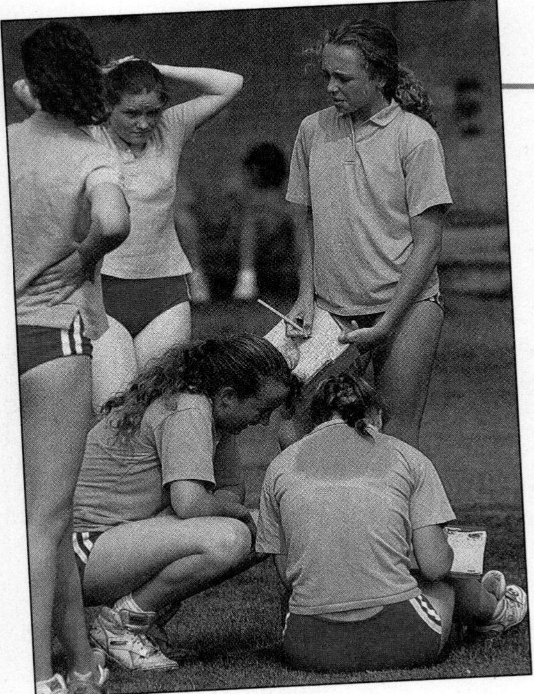

REVIEWING RESULTS

At the end of the set time you can review your programme, using the graphing facilities of the spreadsheet, in order to check the kind of progress you have made. In which activity have you made most progress? Has there been a steady increase in performance, or was there a dramatic improvement after the first few weeks, followed by very little improvement? Whatever the picture shown by the graph, can you explain it?

At set points in the programme you might use the calculating facility of the spreadsheet to analyse the data entered. You could, for example, build up a formula which calculates the total distance which you have run during a particular month. Then build a second formula which calculates the average distance run for each of your training days.

◁ **Fig. 2.23 Recording results**

Fig. 2.24 Measuring a pulse rate ▷

RECALCULATING RESULTS

Once you have put the different formulas into the spreadsheet, why not try out its recalculating facility (this is sometimes called 'What if?')? Imagine that you missed half of your training days and therefore had to enter 0 metres for those days. How much would those days off bring down your average for the month? By how much would you have had to increase your distance on the days on which you did train in order to maintain your original average? Was it possible, given your fitness at the time, to make up for the missed training?

Purpose-made BADGES

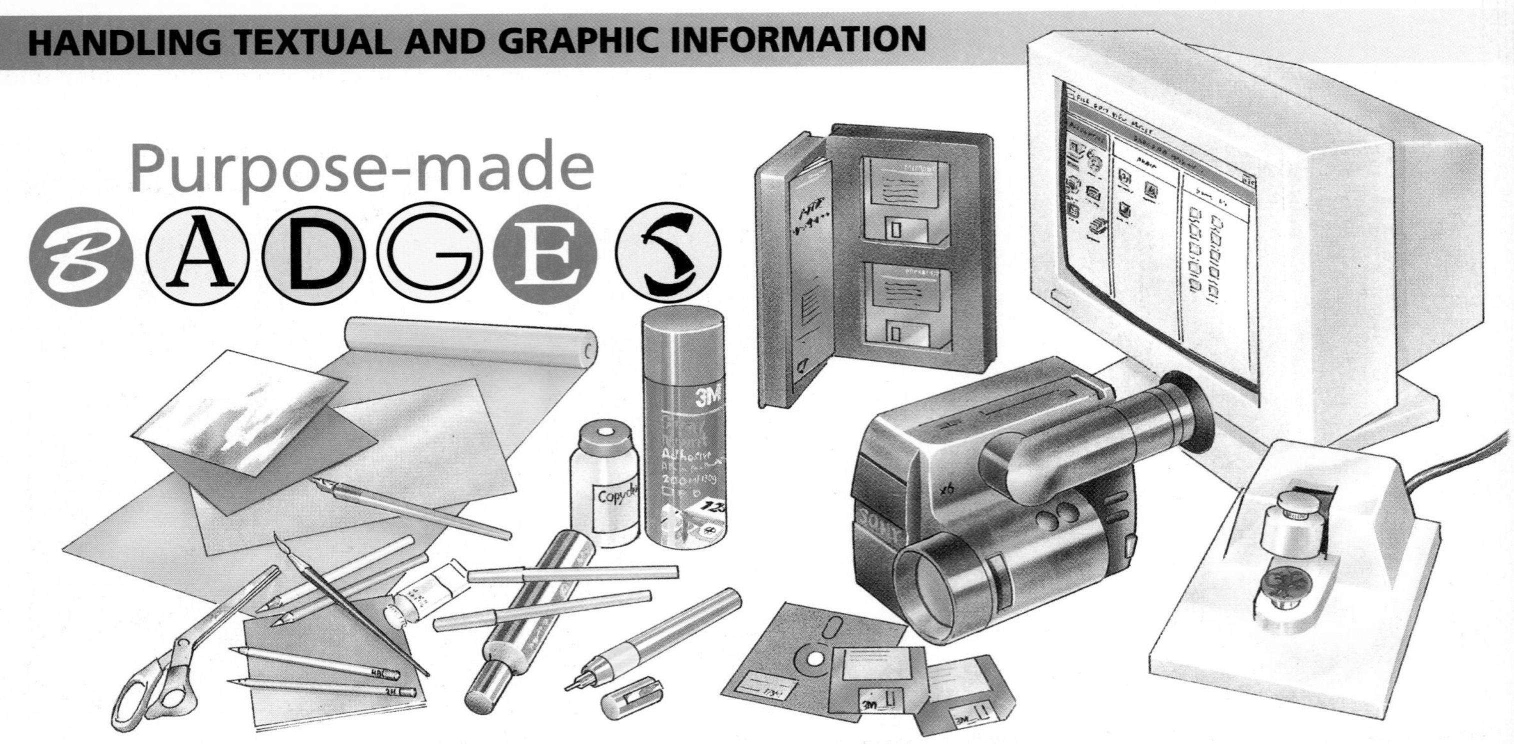

Badge-making is a fun activity and very easy to do. All that is required is paper, a set of coloured pencils and a badge-making machine. But, unless you are a very talented calligrapher or artist, the final product can look very home-made and will probably be quickly thrown away. The tools of Information Technology, however, allow you to create badges which look professional and do not depend upon your being a skilled artist.

There are lots of different types of badges that you can make. Look at the ones in Fig. 2.25. Some use text and simple graphic images to display information. Others have more elaborate designs and silly slogans.

△ **Fig. 2.25**

BADGE BASICS

Whatever kind of information you want on your badge, you will need to choose the kind of software that will help you to achieve what you want. If you want to have text which curls round an image, do you have a piece of software in school which enables you to do that? If you have a range of fonts from which to choose, which one best suits your purpose?

If you want to use graphic information, will you create it on screen, or will you borrow an image from the computer's graphics library or clip art facility? If so, will you need to change its size or shape in any way? Perhaps you would prefer to video your own images and then digitize them? Which would be the most convenient method for you?

Would you need to work in colour, or might black and white images and text printed on to coloured paper be adequate? If you wished to work in colour would the quality of the print-out be satisfactory?

When using IT, you will learn:

that each software item has its own strengths and weaknesses and that the selection of software involves consideration of the facilities offered, ease and simplicity of use, availability and cost

BADGE BONANZA

Badge-making is an activity which you could try out in many different areas of your school work. Here are some suggestions. Can you think of others?

- a badge appropriate to a particular club or organization which its members might wear
- a badge with a memorable slogan to use as part of a campaign to change some aspect of school life or to raise people's awareness of a local environmental issue
- a badge advertising a product or a service which your class is marketing
- a badge protesting against injustice and tyranny

△ **Fig. 2.26**

BADGE BUSINESS

You might be able to provide a badge-making service for the rest of your school as a school-based business. There may even be opportunities for creating a market for your badge service in the local community: a local playgroup, for example, might require hard-wearing, colourful name badges, or a new shop may want to promote itself through badges with a logo and slogan.

△ **Fig. 2.27 Computers can be fitted with a clip art facility.**

△ **Fig. 2.28 Using a video digitizer**

Perhaps you could make several versions of the same slogan, using different fonts and different backgrounds (see Fig. 2.26). Then do some market research to find out the most popular combination of font and background colour.

BADGE BONUS

If you intend to produce a badge which contains an image and text, you might experiment on screen by changing colours, designing different images and altering their size and shape, as well as looking at the most effective way of combining your image with the font.

Once you have decided upon your final version of the badge and have printed it out, all you need to do is put it through your badge-making machine and the result will be an attractive and professional-looking badge.

◁ **Fig. 2.29 Whatever method you use to create your design you will need a badge-making machine.**

△ **Fig. 2.30**

IN THE PLAYGROUP

A playgroup is an ideal place to observe, over a period of time, the development of young children during some of the most important years of their lives. In the pre-school years, children develop at an astonishing rate – in their relationships with other young children, in their physical capability and, above all, in their use of language.

However, remembering every different change in a child from week to week is impossible. To attempt to record them in a notebook as they are happening in front of you is impractical: you are likely to miss so much of what is happening, especially in a large group situation.

USING A VIDEO CAMERA

To capture this kind of information, a video camera is an excellent tool: it can capture a whole scene and store images which can be examined over and over again. It also enables the user to compare images captured over a period of time.

Your group, however, first needs to plan how best to use the video camera. Clearly, if you are trying to capture information about the development of young children over several months you will need to make practical decisions about organization.

When using IT, you will learn:

to work together to prepare and present information using IT

CHOOSING CHILDREN

In consultation with your teacher and the playgroup leader, you will have to decide how often you are going to gather information and for how long. You will then have to agree upon which children to target for your study of child development. Perhaps a variety of different ages would provide a good range of information for discussion.

Finally, you will need to decide which of the many playgroup activities will help with your particular investigation. If you are going to concentrate upon the development of social skills, it would be a good idea to video the child in more than one situation, such as playing with friends and having to sit down to listen to a story.

△ **Fig. 2.31 Choosing who to study**

△ **Fig. 2.32**

If the emphasis in your investigation is upon the language used by a child, a good strategy might be to arrange a series of interviews which allow the child to talk freely about subjects which interest them. On the other hand, you may wish to look closely at the development of such physical skills as running, jumping, catching and kicking.

ANALYSING INFORMATION

Once you have collected together information over a period of time, you will be able to study the videotapes and analyse the scenes which you have shot. What kind of developments did you see in the child? Was its progress very gradual or was there a sudden spurt in its development? Did the changes in the child surprise you, or were you more surprised by a lack of development? Would your findings about child development help you to be a good parent?

Afterwards, you could word process your findings about child development, so that you can present them to the rest of the class.

△ **Fig. 2.33 Months later, studying the tapes**

COME AND LOOK AT MY RECORD COLLECTION

WHAT COULD PAUL HAVE DONE?

Paul was baffled trying to remember just one book which he had been reading only a few weeks ago. If Pam or anyone else had asked him in three months time, he would have remembered even less.

What could Paul have done, so that he didn't have to rely on a faulty memory? He could have written down the title, author and where he found the book on a piece of paper. But over a year he might read an awful lot of football books, so that he would end up with an awful lot of pieces of paper.

Let's imagine that Pam then comes along and asks Paul for a list of books on Manchester United which he has read and enjoyed. He would have to flick through dozens of pieces of paper and then Pam would have to write them out. Slow and very boring.

When using IT, you will learn:

to collect and organize information for entry into a database

to use IT to work more efficiently

SETTING UP A DATABASE

On the other hand, Paul could have kept a record of his football books by making a database of his reading. Even better, he could have set up a database so that everyone in the class could keep a similar record of their own reading. Then he could have published a personal or a class 'top ten' of authors or books.

PAUL'S GUIDE TO DATABASE MAKING

Have a clear idea of why you are making a database, by asking yourself these questions:

- Who is going to use this database?
- Why are they going to use it?

If you haven't got answers to these questions, don't bother.

Choose a database which suits your purpose best:

- If there is a lot of information to store, either now or in the future, you will need a database with a big memory.
- If you want to see the information in the form of graphs and charts, you will need a database which can produce the kinds of graphs and charts which you need.

Once you have decided upon the kind of database you are going to produce, make the following decisions:

- How many records do you need? This might be the number of people in your form, year or even the entire school.
- What fields of information are you going to store so that the database will be useful to as many people as possible?
- Will the information be stored in words, numbers or a mixture of both?

CRIMINAL RECORDS

Tired of the same old software? Fed up with running a business and making a million? Some simulation programs are rather limited. Take a look at the software which you have used in school. Probably each piece of software has its good points: but it will also have some bad ones. If it is a word-processing package, perhaps it doesn't allow you to produce the kind of finished product which you had in mind. If it is a simulation, it may be that you don't find it very realistic or it doesn't allow you enough freedom to make decisions.

Unfortunately, there is nothing you can do to change a particular piece of software. You, and those pupils who use it next year, are stuck with its disadvantages until something better is produced.

But why wait? With a little imagination you can improve some software programs by making your own additions. This is especially true of simulations of real-life situations. Whether it is a program which asks you to decide upon a site for a new supermarket or lead a revolutionary force against a tyrant, you can create extra pieces of software to make the simulation more exciting, more challenging and more fun.

Fig. 2.34 Some simulation programs provide opportunities for expansion.

EXTRA INFORMATION

Most simulations ask you to make decisions. Before you can do this you will need information upon which to base your decisions. The software usually gives information to help the user decide, but you could create extra information which would enable you to reach a greater variety of conclusions.

Imagine, for example, a simulation which asks some of the class to divide themselves up into small groups representing rival newspapers. Most members of the group are reporters who are trying to find out information about a gang of ruthless criminals who have committed an outrageous crime. Other members of the class may be playing the role of the police.

When using IT, you will learn:

to collect and organize information for inputting into a database

to review your use of IT and consider its applications in the outside world

PHOTOS AND FACTS

What kinds of information might you create for the groups to use in their roles as journalists and police officers? What kind of information would be available in this situation and from what sources?

Using the video camera, you might make a series of mug-shots of known criminals. This could include a commentary upon their past activities, who their friends and supporters are and any other information which you think would be appropriate to the simulation. To do this you might use a selection of teachers and friends, suitably dressed-up for the part.

Alternatively, you might use an ordinary camera and a word processor to compile a dossier of bank robbers whose activities are known to the authorities.

Your information and knowledge will shape the content of your video tape or dossier, but remember it must also contain data which relates to the simulation. The information that a criminal uses a false name, for example, would be very helpful.

Name:
Ron Jones

Also Known As:
The Fixer
Peter McGraw

Nationality:
British

Convictions:
7 years for armed robbery

Associates:
Jones has worked alone in the past, although is thought to have masterminded several robberies of building societies in the Birmingham area.

Comments:
He has been in various institutions since the age of four. He finds it difficult to form relationships. Mistrusts all figures of authority.

Category:
'A' Highly Dangerous

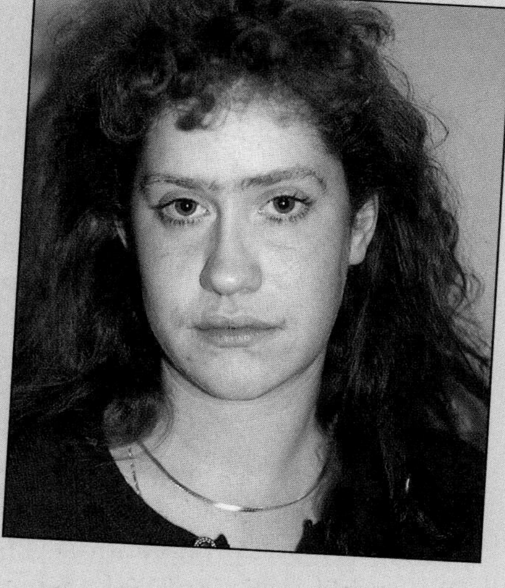

Name:
Anne Woolrich

Also Known As:
Abigail Ward

Nationality:
British

Convictions:
None

Associates:
She has connections with several fringe political organizations, for which she raises funds. Suspected of working with several different gangs of bank robbers as a driver, but no evidence to convict.

Comments:
She is thought to use money stolen in bank robberies to fund illegal political organizations.

Category:
'C' Psychologically Unstable

△ Fig. 2.35

DATABASE DECISIONS

Another source of information might be a database of criminals. If so, you would have to decide on the different fields of information which would be suitable for this type of database. How would the information be used and who would use it? If you are feeling very ambitious, you might make a database in French, German or Spanish, which gives further information on criminal activity in other parts of Europe.

Past, **Present** *and* Future

DATE: THE PAST ☐ PLACE: THE SCHOOL LIBRARY

The pupils are trying to find out information which will be useful for the projects they are starting work on.

One pupil is trying to find out about the origins of the Hindu festival of Diwali. He starts by looking through the index of a set of encylopaedias, tracking down the relevant section in another volume and then copying out any helpful information into a notebook. He then goes to the library catalogue to check and write down the titles and authors of books on the subject.

Another pupil is finding out about the relationship between Great Britain and Germany in the 1930s, as part of a project on the Second World War. She has collected together seven books on European history and is looking through the index for references to the two countries. After quickly reading through these pages of references, she discovers that some are useful and she makes notes. But some are no use at all.

A small group of pupils is looking for information on different careers. They have found a number of books on the subject, but some books seem to contradict each other and many are out of date. How can they tell which is the most reliable source of information?

When using IT, you will learn:

to translate an enquiry expressed in ordinary language into forms required by information retrieval systems

to use search methods to obtain accurate and relevant information from a database

DATE: THE PRESENT AND FUTURE ☐ PLACE: THE SCHOOL RESOURCE CENTRE

The pupils are trying to find out information which will be useful for the project they are starting work on.

One pupil is trying to find out about the origins of the Hindu festival of Diwali. He inserts a CD-ROM disc containing an entire set of encyclopaedias and searches for the entry under 'Hinduism'. Once the information is found, he prints it out. He then goes across to a computer terminal, types in the key word 'Hinduism', and asks the computer to search for any books or articles which are available in the Resource Centre. The computer's search finds three books and a newspaper article containing information on Hinduism.

Fig. 2.36 ▷

△ Fig. 2.37

Another pupil is finding out about the relationship between Great Britain and Germany in the 1930s, as part of a project on the Second World War. She loads a piece of software containing important texts relating to twentieth-century European history. Once the disk is loaded, she types the word 'Britain' and the computer immediately locates a large number of references. To narrow down the field, she then makes a second search by typing in the word 'Germany'. Once the computer has found all the texts which mention the countries together, she prints them out.

A small group of pupils is looking for information on careers. They have listed a number of careers which they wish to investigate, some of which are not available in the locality. They go to the computer and call up on-line databases (as in Fig. 2.38). Using their checklist, they can work quickly through the menus on the screen. Once they have found the relevant screens of information, they download them on to their own work disk. Then they carry out another set of searches, using a different on-line database, to find out useful names and addresses to contact.

SUCCESSFUL SEARCHING

The pupil who was using the CD-ROM and the automated library system was able to find the information he was interested in very quickly and therefore worked more efficiently.

The pupil who was using the electronically stored documents was also able to work much more rapidly because she didn't have to waste time following up useless information. The computer brought together all the relevant information for her.

The group investigating careers didn't have the problem of out-of-date information because they had decided to use databases which would be updated as new information became available.

How do *you* set about tracking down information? Do you make full use of the tools of Information Technology in your project work? When you are planning your work do you think about the most efficient way of collecting information before you start?

△ Fig. 2.38

3 MODELLING

IT IDEAS FOR EACH SUBJECT

Subject	Ideas
English	◇ Participate in a simulation involving the justification of choices, both during the course of the simulation and at the end of it.
Maths	◇ Use a spreadsheeet to model relative frequency. ◆ Use Logo to investigate and analyse geometric shapes **see page 52**.
Science	◆ Use Logo to explore the geometry of the natural world **see page 52**. ◇ Use a spreadsheet to investigate the relationship between force, mass and acceleration.
Technology	◆ Use computer-aided design to model an electronic circuit on screen **see page 50**. ◆ Design a pattern and embroider it on to a piece of fabric using computer-aided manufacture **see page 50**. ◇ Use a spreadsheet to model potential profit margins.
Modern Languages	◇ Participate in an interactive video simulation of a foreign holiday. ◇ Role-play a situation at a foreign hotel's reception desk using CD-ROM.
Geography	◇ Use a spreadsheet to model population change. ◆ Take part in a simulation involving the running of a farm **see page 56**.
History	◆ Take part in a historical simulation **see page 54**.
Art	◆ Evaluate the advantages of computer-aided design in the development of an idea in the classroom and in the commercial world **see page 50**.
PE	◇ Use a spreadsheet to analyse and predict the progressive improvement of world records in track and field events.
RE/PSE	◇ Create a spreadsheet to analyse and predict the decline in Sunday worship. ◇ Participate in a simulation which requires ethical decision-making.
Economic & Industrial Understanding	◇ Investigate the effects of inflation on different household budgets using a spreadsheet. ◆ Use a spreadsheet to calculate value for money **see page 44**.
Careers	◇ Participate in a simulation involving the siting of new industry/business. ◆ Use a spreadsheet to record and monitor a mini-enterprise **see page 48**.
Health	◇ Use a spreadsheet to model the demographic consequences of increased life expectancy as a result of better health care.
Citizenship	◇ Participate in a simulation involving decisions which affect the lives of people in a community, followed by discussion of these decisions. ◆ Use a spreadsheet to model voting patterns **see page 46**.
Environmental Education	◆ Use Logo to investigate the geometric patterns of the local landscape **see page 52**. ◇ Create a spreadsheet to model the impact of progressively increasing volumes of traffic flow upon different points in a town's road system.

Let's pretend

Everyday on television you see wars, elections, summit meetings, company takeovers, and millions of pounds being made and lost. But you can only watch – you can never take part. You can, however, pretend – for years there have been ingenious board games like *Risk* and *Monopoly*.

Now, using Information Technology, you can imitate even more complex situations. This is called modelling.

There are many different reasons for using modelling. Some software models are used to enable people to investigate situations or ideas before putting them into practice for real. Other models are used as an alternative to the real world. They enable people to participate in situations that would otherwise be too dangerous, too expensive or impossible for them to take part in. Consider the following examples of models – which category do they fall into? Do they fall into both?:

- Pilots training to fly aircraft use flight simulators in which they can make decisions (and mistakes) in safety.
- Businesspeople use computer models of their markets to try and calculate how well their product might do in the future, so that they can plan ahead.
- Large furniture stores create graphic models of their kitchen and bathroom designs to ensure that they have made the best use of the available space and so have happy and satisfied customers.

△ **Fig. 3.1 A flight simulator**

Programs similar to these are also available in schools. In your Resource Centre you will probably find a selection of software packages which are models. Sometimes these introduce situations or stories. In order to move the story along you have to interact with the model. You might have to ask the computer questions or make choices from options on the screen. These models are called simulations. They cover a wide range of subjects. There might be adventure models taking you to mythical lands, historical models involving you in important events or geographical models requiring you to make decisions affecting the environment.

Some software allows you to do data modelling: for example, there are spreadsheet programs in which you can enter and manipulate information to help you to investigate various problems and test out ideas.

There are also programs which allow you to create your own simulation, either for members of your class or for the use of other classes in your school.

Whatever program you use, modelling gives you the opportunity to explore uncharted waters without actually getting your feet wet!

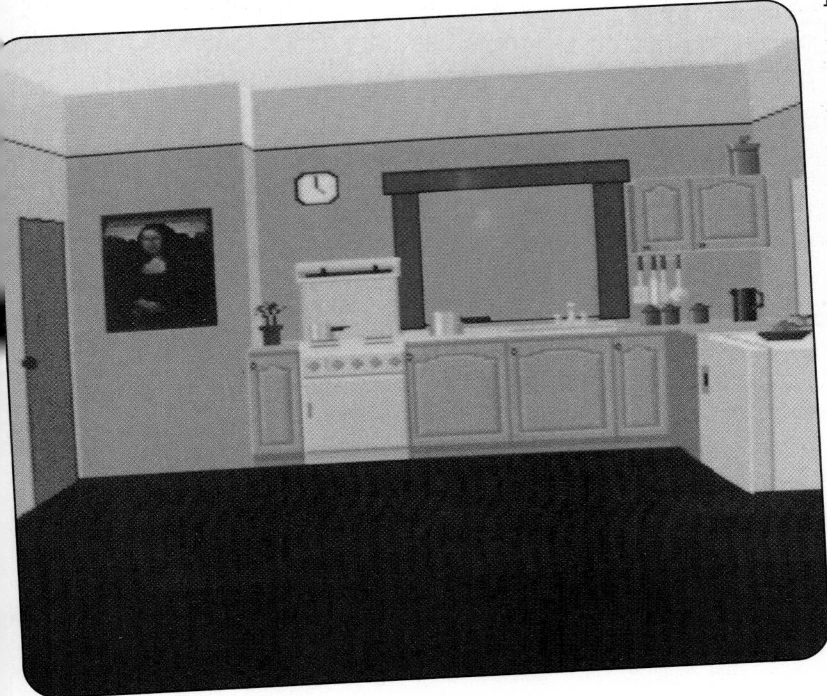

△ **Fig. 3.2 A computer model kitchen**

FOOD *for thought*

Have you ever thought of using Information Technology to help you save money? If your class is well-organized and can also use the facilities of a spreadsheet, the computer is a useful tool for improving the power of the pound in your pocket.

SUPERMARKET CHOICE

Walking round a supermarket and trying to decide what to buy can be a bewildering experience. There is a vast range of goods from which to choose. And, not only are the products often packed in different weights, there are also different brands to choose from. So the customer has to spend quite a lot of time trying to calculate the best buy. For instance, is it cheaper to buy the same brand of cereal in a 500g box or a 750g box? Is it more costly to buy a catering tin of instant coffee or to buy a large number of small jars?

△ **Fig. 3.3 So many things to choose from**

These decisions are made even more difficult by the supermarket changing prices from week to week as it tries to attract buyers. To complicate matters further, different supermarkets in the same area undercut each other's prices to compete against each other.

BEST BUY

By working together in groups it is possible to collect information and, more importantly, to process that information within a spreadsheet in order to work out the best buy, and therefore save money.

First, you will have to decide which items of food you are going to investigate. Try to select a range of products which are bought on a regular basis and are packed in varying weights. Once you have decided which foods to include, enter them into your spreadsheet, along with the different weights of each product and the cost at one particular supermarket. Next, enter a formula into the spreadsheet to calculate the cost of 10 units of the product (a unit could be, for instance, one gram). This will give you a unit cost for each product at each weight, which you can then compare to find out the best buy.

△ **Fig. 3.4**
◁ **Fig. 3.5**
Which is the best buy?

When using IT, you will learn:

to use Information Technology for investigations requiring the analysis of data

PRICE UPDATE

Fig 3.6 shows a spreadsheet that has calculated unit costs: what conclusions can be drawn from the data? Is the biggest packet or jar *always* the best buy? Are the results as you might have predicted?

Once you have set up the spreadsheet, you can nominate a group member each week to go into the supermarket and to report back to school any price changes. These can then be put into the spreadsheet and the unit costs will be automatically recalculated.

If you have more than one supermarket in the area, set up a spreadsheet for the same products on sale in different supermarkets. This way, not only will you be able to keep a check on *what* the best buy is, but also upon *where* the best buy is to be found.

File Edit Formula Format Data Options Macro Window

Normal

G17 | 1/2/1993 12:10 | D15:(C4)©SUM(C15/B15*10)

Spreadsheet 1

	A	B	C	D
1		TESCO CHART		
2	ITEM	WEIGHT	COST	COST/10G
3		grammes		
4				
5	COFFEE	50	£ 0.89	£ 0.1780
6				
7	COFFEE	100	£ 1.59	£ 0.1590
8				
9	COFFEE	300	£ 4.59	£ 0.1530
10				
11	CORNFLAKES	250	£ 0.62	£ 0.0248
12				
13	CORNFLAKES	500	£ 0.76	£ 0.0152
14				
15	CORNFLAKES	750	£ 1.09	£ 0.0145
16				
17				

Ready NUM

△ **Fig. 3.6**

CONSUMER GUIDE

△ **Fig. 3.7**

At the beginning of each week you could word process a consumer guide to basic items of foodstuff, based upon the calculations of your spreadsheet.

Of course, these statistics, though very valuable, will not be the only factors affecting the purchase of foods. To get the full picture of consumer decision-making, you would also have to consider, for example, storage problems, how quickly a large amount of a product will perish, how much cash a family has available to spend on food, and whether it would be more profitable to keep some of the money in a building society, earning interest.

Nevertheless, making accurate comparisons will go a long way towards helping you find value for money.

But what if?

One of the most powerful aspects of a spreadsheet is its ability to instantly calculate and recalculate rows and columns of figures. This capability will help you to do your work much more efficiently, and it will enable you to use your data to create a model on the computer screen.

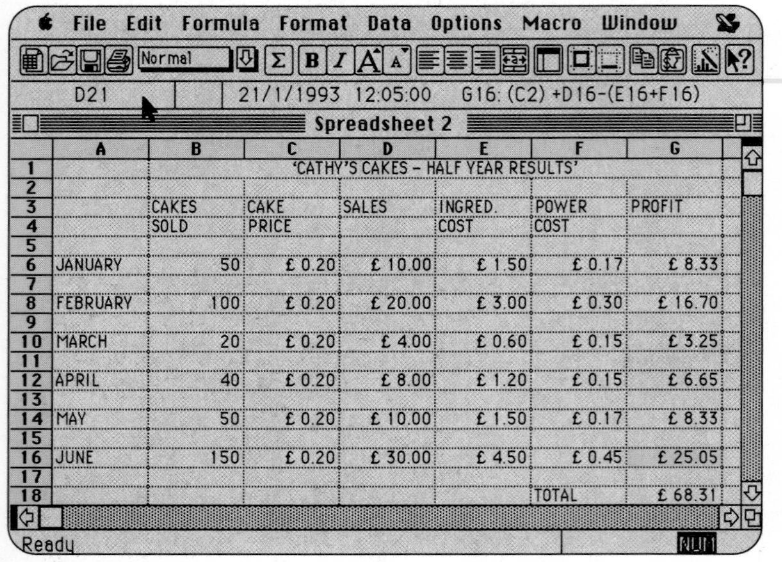

File Edit Formula Format Data Options Macro Window

D21 | 21/1/1993 12:05:00 G16: (C2) +D16-(E16+F16)

Spreadsheet 2

	A	B	C	D	E	F	G
1			'CATHY'S CAKES – HALF YEAR RESULTS'				
2							
3		CAKES	CAKE	SALES	INGRED.	POWER	PROFIT
4		SOLD	PRICE		COST	COST	
5							
6	JANUARY	50	£ 0.20	£ 10.00	£ 1.50	£ 0.17	£ 8.33
7							
8	FEBRUARY	100	£ 0.20	£ 20.00	£ 3.00	£ 0.30	£ 16.70
9							
10	MARCH	20	£ 0.20	£ 4.00	£ 0.60	£ 0.15	£ 3.25
11							
12	APRIL	40	£ 0.20	£ 8.00	£ 1.20	£ 0.15	£ 6.65
13							
14	MAY	50	£ 0.20	£ 10.00	£ 1.50	£ 0.17	£ 8.33
15							
16	JUNE	150	£ 0.20	£ 30.00	£ 4.50	£ 0.45	£ 25.05
17							
18						TOTAL	£ 68.31

Ready NUM

△ **Fig. 3.8**

CAKE CALCULATIONS

In Fig. 3.8 you will see a simple example of how a spreadsheet has been used to make calculations. Cathy has kept a record of how much money she and her brother have earned over the year by baking cakes and selling them. She has entered the data about the money taken each month, and has totalled the income from sales by entering the appropriate formula into the spreadsheet. She has also entered the cost of the ingredients and the cost of the power needed to produce the cakes. Then, with the appropriate formulas entered again, the monthly profit and the final total profit have been automatically calculated by the spreadsheet.

So far Cathy has used the spreadsheet just as a calculator and as a convenient way of capturing and storing data. She might also decide to use the graphing facility of the spreadsheet to investigate any seasonal fluctuations in sales.

FORWARD PLANNING

What would happen to the profit margin if Cathy and her brother put up the price of their cakes in the second half of the year? By using the modelling facility of the spreadsheet, Cathy will be able to predict the answer to this question. If she alters the data in the appropriate column for the appropriate months, the spreadsheet will recalculate any figures affected by the change. For example, if they put up the price in July by 10 per cent, and the same number of cakes were made and sold in the second half of the year, the spreadsheet would calculate that the profit for the second half of the year would be £76.51 rather than £68.31.

When using IT, you will learn:

to modify the data and rules of a computer model

ELECTION CAMPAIGN

The asking of 'What if?' questions has applications in many different areas. One very important situation in which it is used is in a General Election campaign, where changing statistics may mean different voting patterns – and possibly a change of government.

You have probably seen television programmes in which politicians and interviewers talk about different voting patterns. You may have seen them make projections about what would happen if there were changes in attitude by the voters. Just like Cathy who was modelling what would happen if she and her brother increased the price of their cakes, politicians and interviewers might ask what would happen if there were a 2.5 per cent swing against the government across the whole country – or just certain parts of the country. Alternatively, if a particular issue like unemployment or homelessness became important to voters, how far would this determine the course of an election?

All these important questions are answered by careful research and analysis; but until the votes are counted, the verdicts are only projections, based upon computer models of what the situation might be.

△ **Fig. 3.9**

ELECTION SPREADSHEET

Why not produce your own election spreadsheet, based either upon real or imaginary data about the number of votes for different parties in different constituencies, as in Fig. 3.10? Ask the spreadsheet:

- ○ What if Labour increased its vote by 5% in Sarum in the next election?
- ○ What if 1% of Old Leeke's Liberal Democrat voters had stayed at home?
- ○ What if Milton West's Green candidate took 15% of Labour's vote?

File Edit Formula Format Data Options Macro Window

N10 3/2/1993 12:21 PM F8: ©SUM(D8-C8)

Spreadsheet 4

	A	B	C	D	E	F
1	CONSTITUENCY		NUMBER OF VOTES FOR PARTY			
2						
3						
4		CON	LABOUR	LIB. DEM.	GREEN	MAJORITY
5						
6	Sarum	17321	15999	6001	750	1322
7						
8	Old Leeke	2003	9271	9561	4017	290
9						
10	Milton West	3336	9011	10311	9011	1300
11						
12						

Ready

△ **Fig. 3.10**

If you are interested in *why* people vote the way they do, you might set up a spreadsheet with some imaginary data concerning election issues, as in Fig. 3.11. Once again, you could model various situations:

- ○ What if the number of votes for all parties on the defence issue were halved?
- ○ What if Labour had concentrated on environmental issues, and had taken three quarters of the Green votes on this issue?

You might even put together a short Election Special television programme, in which the politicians and interviewer discuss your projections and the election chances of the government. Why not word process a script for the programme?

File Edit Formula Format Data Options Macro Window

L16 15/1/1993 05:20 G13: [W7] ©SUM(B13..F13)

Spreadsheet 3

	A	B	C	D	E	F	G
1	NUMBER OF PEOPLE VOTING FOR EACH PARTY BECAUSE OF A PARTICULAR ISSUE						
2	CONSTITUENCY: BLETCHLEY						
3	CONSERVATIVE MAJORITY = 1320						
4							
5		Housing	Education	Employment	Defence	Environment	Total
6							
7	CON	4000	3000	3000	5000	1321	16321
8							
9	LABOUR	6000	5000	2001	1000	1000	15001
10							
11	LIB. DEM.	1500	1141	1000	900	1050	5591
12							
13	GREEN	40	60	150	100	2000	2350
14							
15	LOONY	10	30	5	2	15	62
16							
17							
18							
19							

Ready

△ **Fig. 3.11**

mini-MANAGEMENT

Running a school bookshop, tuckshop or any kind of school-based business involves all kinds of calculations and responsibilities. Information Technology can help you keep your records up-to-date and decide what changes need to be made.

It is important, as in the business world, to keep exact records of transactions so that money can be properly accounted. A spreadsheet is a useful tool both for keeping accounts and for monitoring the progress of your business.

◁ **Fig. 3.12 Running the School Shop**

CALCULATING WITH A SPREADSHEET

Have a look at the spreadsheet in Fig. 3.13. The pupils have been growing different seedlings in the school greenhouse which they sell to the teachers and parents. They have kept a record of the sales of individual plants during the course of a week and, at the same time, a record of the total sales. It would have been possible to work out all these figures on a calculator and to write the answer down on a piece of paper. Deciding to use a spreadsheet, however, has given the pupils several valuable advantages:

File Edit Formula Format Data Options Macro Window

Normal

G17 | 20/3/1993 05:02 | D11: (C2) ©SUM(D5..D9)

Spreadsheet 5

	A	B	C	D
1				
2		UNIT	NUMBER	SALES
3		PRICE	SOLD	
4				
5	MARIGOLD	£ 0.10	100	£ 10.00
6				
7	LOBELIA	£ 0.20	200	£ 40.00
8				
9	ALYSSUM	£ 0.05	200	£ 10.00
10				
11			TOTAL	£ 60.00
12				
13				
14				
15				
16				
17				

Ready NUM

△ **Fig. 3.13**

When using IT, you will learn:

to use IT for investigations requiring the analysis of data

to design a computer model for a specific purpose

- Once the formula is in the spreadsheet, the computer will do all the calculations automatically.
- The pupils can see at a glance which aspects of their business are most or least successful.
- At the end of term the group can print out graphs and statistics about their business and make plans for next year.

MODELLING WITH A SPREADSHEET

Now, have a look at the spreadsheet in Fig. 3.14. Here the pupils have been running a school tuckshop. Like the first group they realize that the spreadsheet might help them to monitor how well the business is going. But they have also discovered that by setting up the spreadsheet in a different way, they can do more than the first group. By inputting more data and entering appropriate formulas, they can use the computer to model possible future situations and then base new plans on these results.

File Edit Formula Format Data Options Macro Window

Normal

M13 2/2/1993 12:20 PM E20:(C2) ©SUM(E14..E19)

Spreadsheet 6

	A	B	C	D	E
1	ITEM	PURCHASE	NUMBER	UNIT	NUMBER
2		PRICE/BOX	ITEMS PER	SELLING	SOLD
3			BOX	PRICE	WEEK 1
4	Milky Way	£ 4.35	48	£ 0.12	34
5	Polos	£ 3.54	48	£ 0.10	26
6	KitKat	£ 4.79	72	£ 0.10	34
7	Chewits	£ 2.65	36	£ 0.10	44
8	Crisps	£ 4.68	48	£ 0.14	200
9	Soft Drinks	£ 2.49	24	£ 0.20	100
10					
11	NUMBER	NUMBER	NUMBER	MONTHLY	PROFIT
12	SOLD	SOLD	SOLD	TOTAL	
13	WEEK 2	WEEK 3	WEEK 4		
14	45	22	56	157	£ 4.61
15	47	34	56	163	£ 4.28
16	87	98	58	277	£ 9.27
17	35	50	27	156	£ 4.12
18	240	290	340	1070	£ 45.48
19	145	179	123	547	£ 52.65
20				TOTAL	£ 120.41

Ready NUM

△ **Fig. 3.14**

QUESTIONS AND ANSWERS

Once the pupils have set up the appropriate labels, data and formulas, they can monitor their business as it progresses. But they can also ask a range of questions about the future and get answers from the computer:

- What should the selling price be if the cost price of a certain product went up by 10 per cent? Would the business have to up the selling price by the whole 10% in order to make a profit?
- What if the local corner shop cut its prices by 5 per cent? Could the business compete successfully by doing the same?

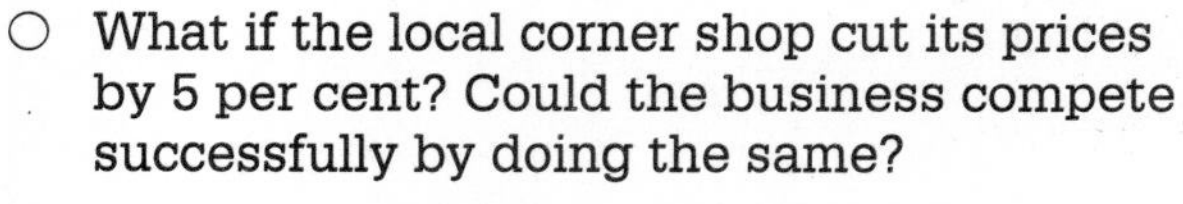

- Would it be a good idea to cut the price of the least popular item in the school tuckshop, hoping that this would boost sales?

The information gathered from asking these questions and modelling them on the computer screen is useful in making future plans. But, just as in the real world, it is not the whole story and will be used alongside other information sources, such as market research and advertising. However, having the computer projections to hand will enable these pupils to speak with confidence and authority about the future of their school-based businesses.

SCREEN TESTS

When you set out to design something you often find that producing a design proposal can be a long-drawn-out process. You will probably generate a lot of sketches to try out different modifications of your ideas. Using a computer you can develop and test your ideas on screen quickly and effectively.

COMPUTER-AIDED DESIGN

Designing on a computer screen is known as computer-aided design (CAD). CAD is used for a variety of tasks. When architects are making plans for new buildings, they often use a computer to model their designs on screen. They input information about size, colour and the position of the proposed building, which the computer converts into a graphic image. Similarly, kitchen designers use modelling programs to explore the various options open to them when fitting a kitchen. In both cases, the computer can produce a 3-D colour image for the designer to consider. If the architect or kitchen designer is not satisfied, the model on screen can easily be altered or adjusted.

△ Fig. 3.15

△ Fig. 3.16

When using IT, you will learn:

to use Information Technology to work more effectively

that Information Technology can be used to do things which can also be done in other ways

In school, you probably won't get the chance to use CAD programs as powerful as those used by professional architects and kitchen designers. However, you will have various CAD programs in your software library which will enable you to model ideas on the screen.

USING CAD IN SCHOOL

You could perform a variety of tasks using CAD. A drawing program, for instance, could help you model ideas for a fabric design, as in Fig. 3.17. Another program might provide you with a screen model of a simple electronic circuit that you can modify, as in Fig. 3.18. Or, if you were doing a project on transport, you could use a program which enables you to model a design for a car on the screen, as in Fig. 3.19.

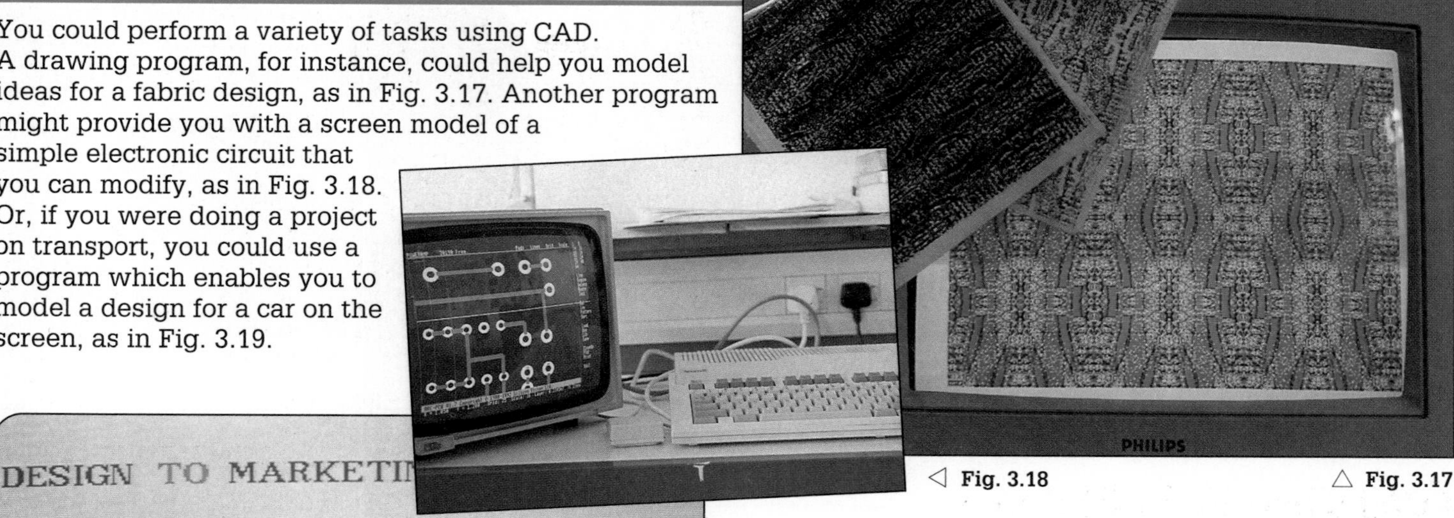

◁ Fig. 3.18

△ Fig. 3.17

COMPUTER-AIDED MANUFACTURE

Closely related to the idea of CAD is computer-aided manufacture (CAM), whereby a computer is used to control machines as part of the making process. This application of Information Technology has been used for many years in industry. However, there are probably opportunities at school for you to use CAM. Perhaps you have a computer-controlled sewing machine which can help you to embroider patterns on fabrics, as in Fig. 3.20.

◁ Fig. 3.19

COMPUTER NUMERICAL CONTROL

Alternatively, you may be able to use a kind of CAD manufacture called computer numerical control (CNC). (The process is given this name because it uses programs written as a series of numbers to operate the machines.) You may have a computer-controlled lathe or milling machine at school which uses CNC. This application of the tools of Information Technology will enable you to design an object on screen and then make it using appropriate software and computer-controlled machines.

CAD, CAM and CNC are all ways of making the design and manufacturing processes efficient and quick. There are always alternative ways of working. On these pages you have been shown ways of creating designs and modelling ideas on a screen. Think of the alternative ways of generating these designs and ideas. What advantages does the use of a computer have over these other ways of working?

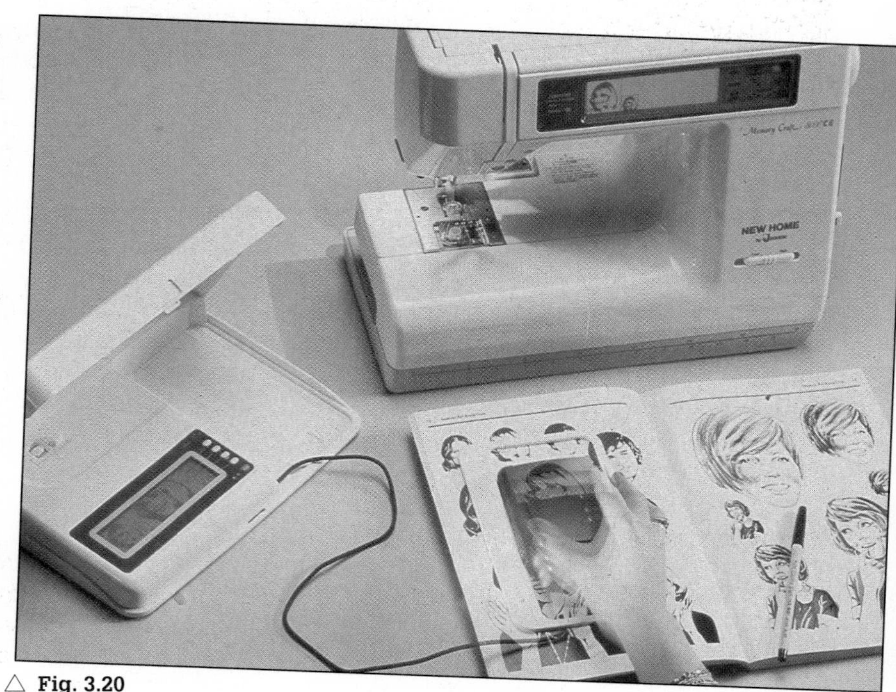

△ Fig. 3.20

GOING LOGO

DRAW ME AN ISOSCELES TRIANGLE!

A computer is a very obedient creature. If you give it instructions, it will do as you ask. However, you need to communicate with a computer in a language which it can understand, otherwise it will get confused and won't be able to carry out the task you have set it. The list of instructions given to a computer is called a program.

Not only does the computer need to understand the language in which the program is given; the order of the instructions is crucial too. If the instructions are in the wrong order, then, again, the computer will get confused. Just like people, computers can follow instructions efficiently only if they are in a precise and logical sequence.

△ **Fig. 3.21 Creating shapes on screen**

LOGO LANGUAGE

There is a wide range of programming languages. A very simple one which you will probably come across in school is called 'Logo'.

Logo enables the user to construct combinations of different shapes on screen by giving instructions to a screen 'turtle'. In Fig. 3.22 you will see an example of Logo language. Here, the user is asking the computer to draw a simple shape on the screen. The instructions are in short, logical steps, telling the turtle to move in particular directions, for particular distances, to create a shape with specific dimensions.

PRECISION AND EFFICIENCY

Using the Logo program is an extremely effective way of creating geometric shapes because the computer is very precise and efficient in constructing lines and angles. Although drawing one square with a protractor, pencil, ruler and paper may be a short and manageable task, what if you want to repeat the same shape thirty times over? It would be very tedious to do that by hand, but you could use the computer to perform the task just by instructing it to repeat the program thirty times.

FD 100	*FD 100 means move forward 100 units.*
RT 90	*RT 90 means turn 90 degrees to the right.*
FD 100	
RT 90	
FD 100	
RT 90	
FD 100	

△ **Fig. 3.22 Can you tell what shape is being made?**

When using IT, you will learn:

to analyse the patterns and relationships in a computer model to establish how its rules operate; change the rules and predict the effect

to write a simple computer program for a particular purpose

CREATING SHAPES

You can use Logo to create geometrical shapes which are as simple or as complex as you wish. The only limit to your use of Logo is your imagination.

Think of the natural world and the fantastic variety of shapes in it. Can you think of examples from the natural environment whose structures are regular geometrical shapes, or look like a combination of regular geometrical shapes? If so, can you reproduce those shapes on screen by using Logo?

◁ Fig.3.23

△ Fig. 3.24

If you live in a town or city, look at the urban skyline. What kind of shapes combine together to form what you see? Could you reproduce that skyline using the Logo program?

◁ Fig. 3.25

LOGO FOR ALL SUBJECTS

Your explorations of the geometry of the natural and urban environments might be used in several different subject areas.

They could, for instance, be used as a basis for a painting or a design project. If your Logo program has facilities for producing coloured lines, you could experiment with various colour combinations on screen (as in Fig. 3.26). There are worksheets for helping you explore the shapes possible with Logo (Fig. 3.27). Your new shapes might give you ideas and images for writing a poem.

Whatever your use of the Logo program, the print-outs of your screen explorations will be useful material for a presentation about how your ideas grew and developed. Alternatively, you might combine your designs with word-processed text as a piece of desk-top publishing.

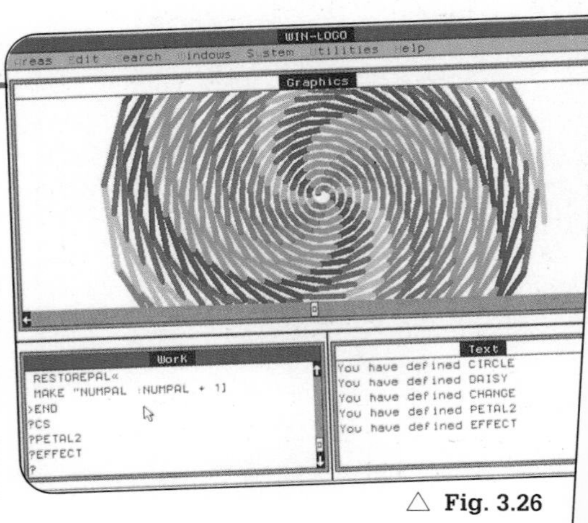

△ Fig. 3.26

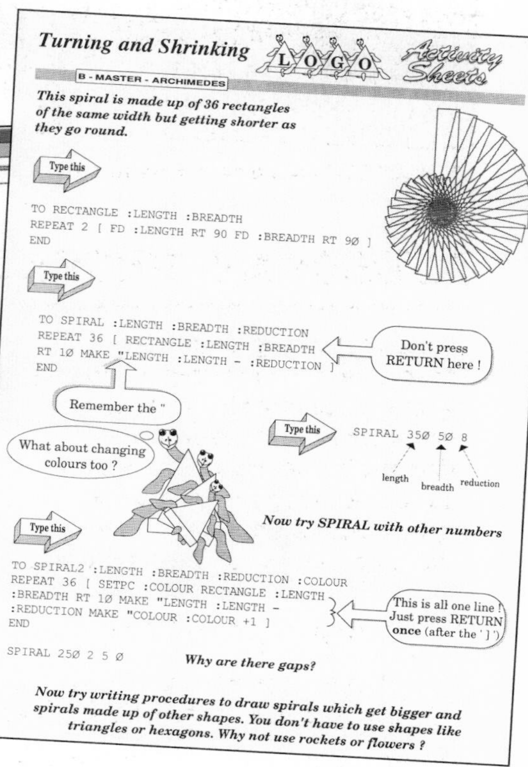

Turning and Shrinking LOGO Activity Sheets

B - MASTER - ARCHIMEDES

This spiral is made up of 36 rectangles of the same width but getting shorter as they go round.

Type this

```
TO RECTANGLE :LENGTH :BREADTH
REPEAT 2 [ FD :LENGTH RT 90 FD :BREADTH RT 9Ø ]
END
```

Type this

```
TO SPIRAL :LENGTH :BREADTH :REDUCTION
REPEAT 36 [ RECTANGLE :LENGTH :BREADTH
RT 1Ø MAKE "LENGTH :LENGTH - :REDUCTION ]
END
```

Don't press RETURN here !

Remember the "

What about changing colours too ?

Type this

```
SPIRAL 35Ø 5Ø 8
```

length breadth reduction

Now try SPIRAL with other numbers

Type this

```
TO SPIRAL2 :LENGTH :BREADTH :REDUCTION :COLOUR
REPEAT 36 [ SETPC :COLOUR RECTANGLE :LENGTH
:BREADTH RT 1Ø MAKE "LENGTH :LENGTH -
:REDUCTION MAKE "COLOUR :COLOUR +1 ]
END
```

This is all one line ! Just press RETURN once (after the '] ')

```
SPIRAL 25Ø 2 5 Ø
```

Why are there gaps?

Now try writing procedures to draw spirals which get bigger and spirals made up of other shapes. You don't have to use shapes like triangles or hexagons. Why not use rockets or flowers ?

△ Fig. 3.27

LIVING IN THE PAST

Have you ever thought of using a computer as a time machine? Computer simulations can transport you into the past so that you can 'take part' in aspects of life as it used to be lived.

Have a look in your software library to see what kind of historical simulations are available for you to use.

△ Fig. 3.28

STRATEGIC THINKING

Some simulations ask you to imagine yourself in a specific historical situation, such as the Bolshevik Revolution, or a crucial battle in the First World War. This type of simulation requires you to work out strategies for dealing with problems as they unfold on the computer screen – problems similar to those faced by leaders during the actual events. By choosing from a series of options on the screen you can affect the outcome and rewrite history!

△ **Fig. 3.29 Discussion is important throughout a simulation.**

ROLE-PLAY

Other simulations require you to role-play the part of someone living in the past. You may be a member of a family living through the terrible events of the Black Death, or you could be sailing to America with Christopher Columbus. In this type of simulation you are asked to make decisions about your life and the lives of others. Your decisions are then fed into the computer and their consequences flashed up on the screen.

A good deal of the action in this kind of simulation takes place away from the computer, in discussion between members of a group, each playing their parts. Each individual has a point of view to contribute and must be heard, and these points of view must be taken into account before firm decisions are made. You might add a dramatic dimension to the simulation by dressing up in the costume of the period which is appropriate to your role.

When using IT, you will learn:

to analyse the patterns and relationships in a computer model to establish how its rules operate; change the rules and predict the effect

KEEP A DIARY

During the simulation you might keep notes recording your thoughts and feelings as each decision is made. This could form the basis of a diary written by the character whom you were playing, either during or after the events.

When the simulation is over, discuss with your teacher and the rest of the class the kinds of pressures which you felt yourself under. Were you acting out of selfish motives or were you taking others into account? Most importantly, did participating in the simulation help you to understand the lives of people in the past? If it did help you to empathize with them, how did the experience differ from just reading about the events in a textbook?

△ **Fig. 3.30 This simulation will take you on an archaeological dig.**

△ **Fig. 3.31 How do simulations compare with textbooks?**

HISTORY TOUR

Another kind of historical simulation creates a situation in which you can talk to a character from the past. You are able to ask questions about what life was like for the Aztecs or during the English Civil War (see Fig. 3.32). At the same time, the character from the past will guide you through various parts of their world, using pictures on the screen and answering questions on the way. This type of historical simulation allows you to interact with the computer by using natural language rather than by making a choice from a few options on the screen.

If you have experienced both kinds of simulations, compare them. What advantages does one have over the other? Which type did you find more effective in helping you to understand various aspects of the past? How might they be improved? Are historical simulations more powerful when they involve role-play, rather than just sitting in front of the computer screen?

the gods!
Wait! I have not made my daily sacrifice... I must find a cactus needle... ah yes, there's one... ouch!.. I have pricked my finger and let a drop of blood fall to the ground... so, we can continue now.
why did you do that?
We all make this sacrifice every day. We feed the gods of the earth with a little of our blood, so that they will continue to feed us with new crops.
what is a chinampa?
The chinampa is our home. It is an island, made by piling up plants and mud from the lake. The edges of the chinampa are held in place by wooden posts. Here and there my father has planted trees to help hold the soil together.
get into the canoe
I am getting in... I am in the canoe now and pushing off... I am paddling towards the causeway... I am getting out of the canoe. Now I ...

and ruts just here, where the cows' hooves churn up the mud. I can see the mill in the distance to the east.
Where are you?
I am by the yard gate.
Describe the mill
Very well, wait now ...
I am by the mill.
Describe the mill
The mill is a tall, handsome building, built from stone from Pibsbury quarry. 'Tis powered by a stream that comes down from Ham Down. The water rushes down the hill and turns the great mill wheel - I likes just standing and watching the water froth and foam.
Our teazel field is to the south.
what is a teazel?
Teazels are a tall plant. Their heads are covered in little, sharp hooks. When the heads are ripe, they're cut off and sent up the river, to be sold to cloth-makers. I'm not too sure what the cloth-makers use them for - I think its to comb the wool and make it smooth.

Fig. 3.32 ▷

GEOGRAPHY *without tears*

Using simulation software can help you to develop a number of important skills, such as decision-making, working with a group of other people and problem-solving. It also allows you and other members of the class to get involved in situations which, in the real world, would be too dangerous, too costly, or even impossible.

DEALING WITH DISASTERS

Only a very reckless Geography teacher would take you on field trips which risked serious injury or death. Climbing into volcanoes or through the rubble of falling buildings would be a novel way of learning about natural disasters, but it would be a worry for your parents! Experiencing any dangerous natural phenomenon at first-hand, whether it is a volcano, a hurricane or radiation, is out of the question. But being part of a computer simulation can, with a little imagination, bring you closer to the real thing.

△ Fig. 3.33

◁ Fig. 3.34

When using IT, you will learn:

- *to analyse the patterns and relationships in a computer model to establish how its rules operate; change the rules and predict the effect*
- *modify the data and rules of a computer model*

LOOK BEFORE YOU LEAP

Some simulations involve the users in events which in real life might be very costly. These models allow you to participate in situations without having to run the real risks of losing either your money or someone else's money.

You could find yourself in charge of an inquiry to find the best site for a new supermarket, or you might be asked to construct the best route for a new railway system. In both cases, in the real world bad decisions can involve a serious loss of money. The computer model allows you the luxury of making poor decisions without these serious consequences. You can go through the same simulation several times until you have got it right. This is not always possible in real life: often your first chance is also your last.

WORK EXPERIENCE

Would you make a good farmer? There is a program which involves your making decisions about the running of a farm. Here you might be faced with a number of decisions about the kind of crops which you are going to plant in a single year, or over a series of years. You would have to take into account a number of variable factors such as climate and rainfall. Just like the farmer in real life, you will be using your meteorological and geographical knowledge to analyse the situation before making firm decisions.

Alternatively, you might be asked to run a business over a period of time, in competition against other businesses run by people in your class. This would mean deciding what to spend your money on in order to make the most profit.

Maypole Farm - East England

1 50ha
2 40ha
3 20ha
4 15ha
5 10ha

Year 4

WEATHER
Warm & wet

FIELD	PROFIT
1	£ 4720
2	£ 4860
3	£ 5180
4	£ 17250
5	£ 1225
	£ 33235

AVERAGE for last 4 years
£ 28095

Press SPACE BAR to continue

△ Fig. 3.35

Whatever type of simulation you are using, remember that your decisions affect the progress of the simulation and, unlike computer games, there is no one correct solution. Remember also that decisions must be made carefully, taking into account a number of viewpoints. To enter decisions randomly and carelessly into the computer defeats the object of using the simulation.

ANALYSING DECISIONS

If your simulation involves statistical work, you might record and analyse the results of your decisions by entering them on to a spreadsheet. This would give you information during the course of the simulation upon which you could base the next set of decisions.

The model doesn't end as soon as you switch off your computer. At the end of any kind of simulation, it is important to discuss with your teacher and the entire class just why you made your decisions. It might therefore be a good idea to give a member of your group the responsibility of noting down reasons for each decision. It would probably make very interesting reading afterwards.

4 MEASUREMENT AND CONTROL

IT IDEAS FOR EACH SUBJECT

Subject	Ideas
English	◇ Give a series of clear instructions to a human 'robot'.
Maths	◇ Control a screen turtle to create geometric shapes using Logo.
Science	◆ Write a program for a computer system to control a sequence of lights on a control interface **see page 60.** ◆ Log experimental data such as time and temperature using sensors or a spreadsheet **see page 64**.
Technology	◆ Control the movements of a floor turtle **see page 62**. ◇ Build and control models of lock-gates or a railway crossing. ◇ Manufacture fabric using a computer-programmed weaving machine. ◇ Use a computer-controlled lathe or milling machine.
Modern Languages	◇ Give a series of clear instructions to a human 'robot' in the target language to carry out a simple task.
Geography	◆ Consider the uses of satellites in gathering information about the Earth's land, sea and atmosphere **see page 72**. ◆ Analyse weather patterns using information provided by satellite images **see page 74**.
Art	◇ Program a floor turtle or a screen turtle to draw a simple picture.
Music	◆ Use a keyboard, MIDI interface and computer to create a jingle to advertise a particular product **see page 68**.
PE	◆ Assess your recovery rate by using sensors to monitor heart and lung performance **see page 66**.
RE/PSE	◇ Discuss the ethical implications of the use of IT to detect disease or abnormalities in the unborn child.
Economic & Industrial Understanding	◇ Consider the use of IT for stock control in retail outlets (eg. bar-code scanners in supermarkets).
Health	◇ Consider the uses and implications of electronic devices such as pacemakers and hospital scanners.
Environmental Education	◆ Use sensors to control an automated watering system in a greenhouse **see page 70**.

Under control

When you hear about computers which control things, perhaps you think of robots that you have seen on the television or in films. But computers can control much more than just robots. They are used in many different situations for the purpose of measuring and controlling. The photographs on this page illustrate a variety of those situations.

A hospital uses computer scanners and sensors to monitor and measure a patient's condition. The computer displays these measurements on screen and can sound alarms if the patient is in any danger.

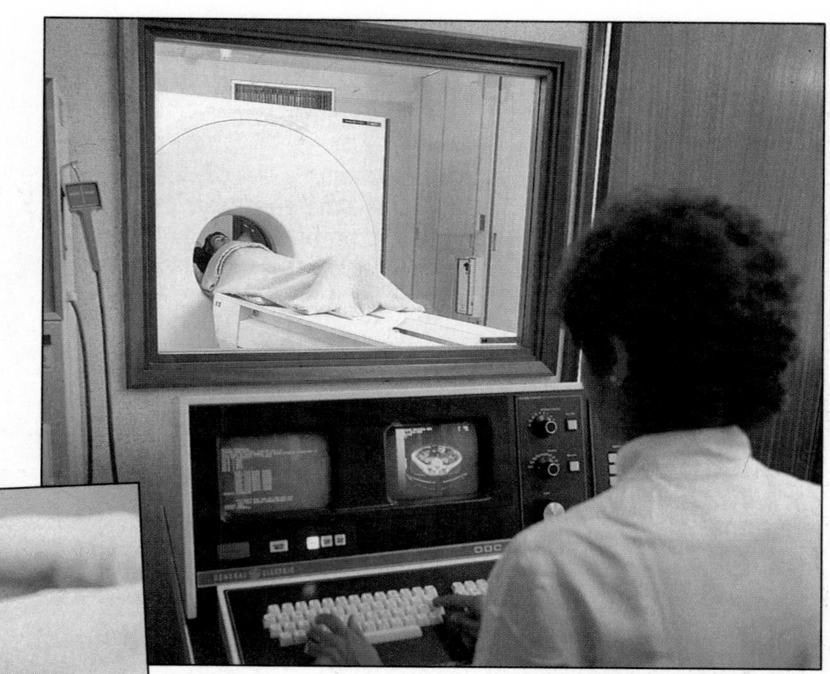

△ **Fig. 4.1 Brain scanner**

△ **Fig. 4.2 Supermarket checkout**

On the High Street we encounter computers all the time. Cash registers do much more than add up your purchases and present you with a bill. When the assistant uses a scanner to read the bar code, the computer can record how many of those particular items have been bought and how many are left in stock. The store manager will then be able to see at a glance when to order new stock; or the computer can be programmed to send out order forms when stocks fall below pre-set levels.

There are also very complex computer systems helping to bring us the daily weather forecasts we see on television. These systems are used to control the satellites from which meteorologists get the information for their reports.

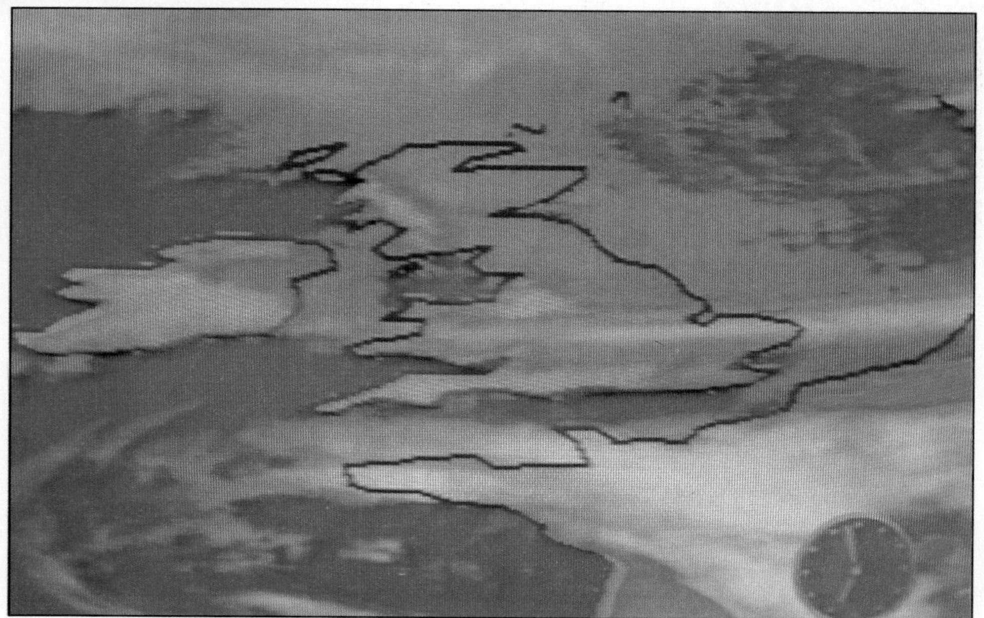

Fig. 4.3 Computerized television weather map ▷

LIGHT SHOWS

Whenever you have to give someone else a set of instructions, it is important that those instructions are both simple and clear. If they are too complicated or obscure in any way you will fail to communicate, and the person you have given instructions to will do something wrong.

Similarly, when using a computer to switch devices on and off you need to be very clear and precise with your instructions – otherwise the device will not do what you want it to do.

TRAFFIC LIGHTS

The importance of having these clear instructions (also known as programs) can be seen every day on the street when you approach a set of traffic lights in a car or on your bike. A set of traffic lights not only has to follow its own sequence correctly. At crossroads, for example, it also has to work in conjunction with the other set of lights. So you can imagine that if the program controlling the sequence of lights were faulty, the result would be chaos. There would be confusion about who had the right of way and cars would be colliding into each other.

Fortunately, the computer controlling the lights ensures that they go through the same repeated sequence of colours all day. When red is on the drivers must stop. Red is joined by amber and the drivers can get ready to move. Both red and amber are turned off and green is turned on: the drivers can now move off. The next part of the instruction turns off the green and turns on the amber. The drivers are warned that the signal to stop is about to be turned on. In the final stage of the sequence, amber is turned off and the red is turned on. The drivers stop.

KEEP IT SIMPLE

All road users know and understand the continuous sequence of lights at a traffic control which have just been described. However, a computer needs even simpler statements. We can set out the instructions as very simple statements arranged in order, as in Fig. 4.4.

When using IT, you will learn:

that programmable devices can be controlled using sequences of instructions

that the order in which instructions are presented, and the form in which they are given to a computer is important

to write a simple computer program for a particular purpose

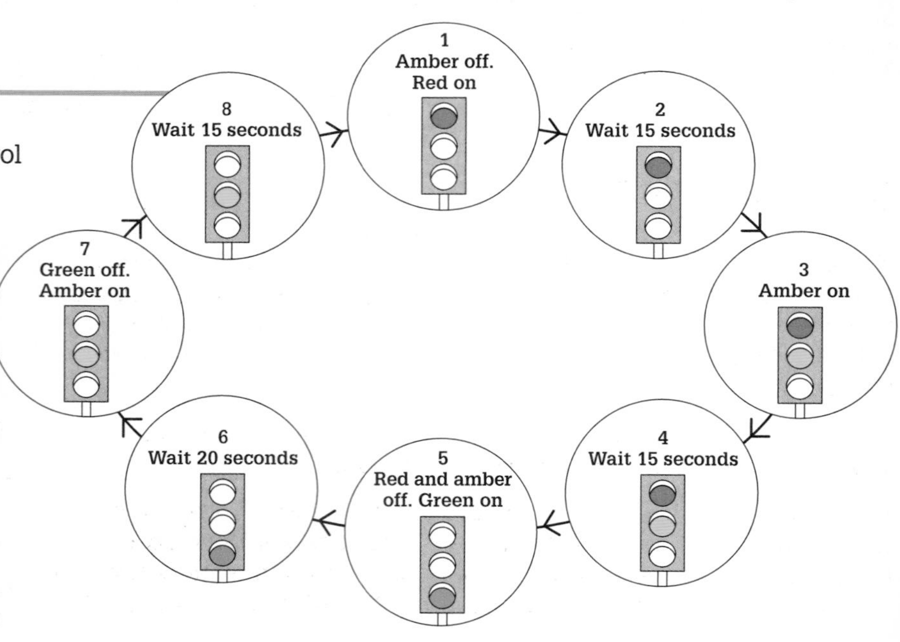

△ **Fig. 4.4**

LIGHT CONTROL

Using a computer system, a control interface (like the one in Fig. 4.5) and an appropriate program from your software library, you can set up your own set of traffic lights. Try to find a way to time the pause between the light changes. As the timing of the lights' phases are very similar, can the operation be simplified and can it be repeated?

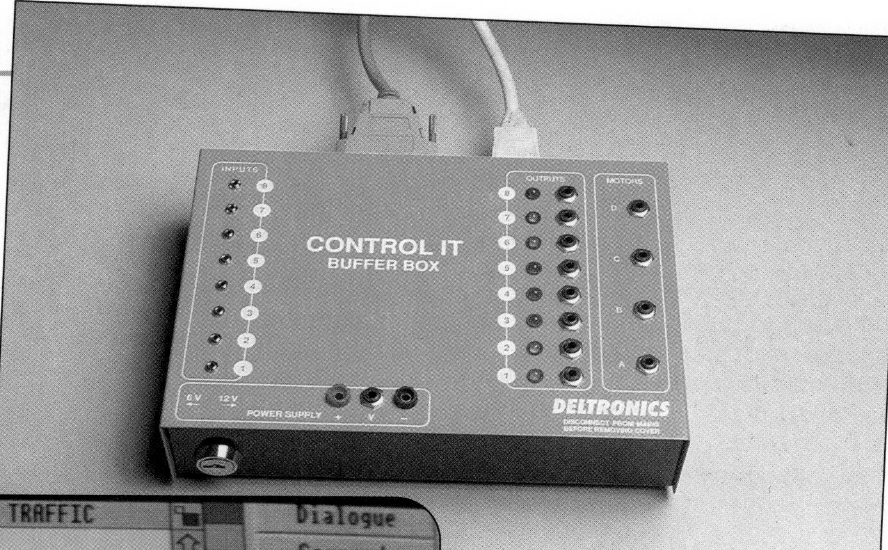

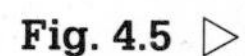

Fig. 4.5 ▷

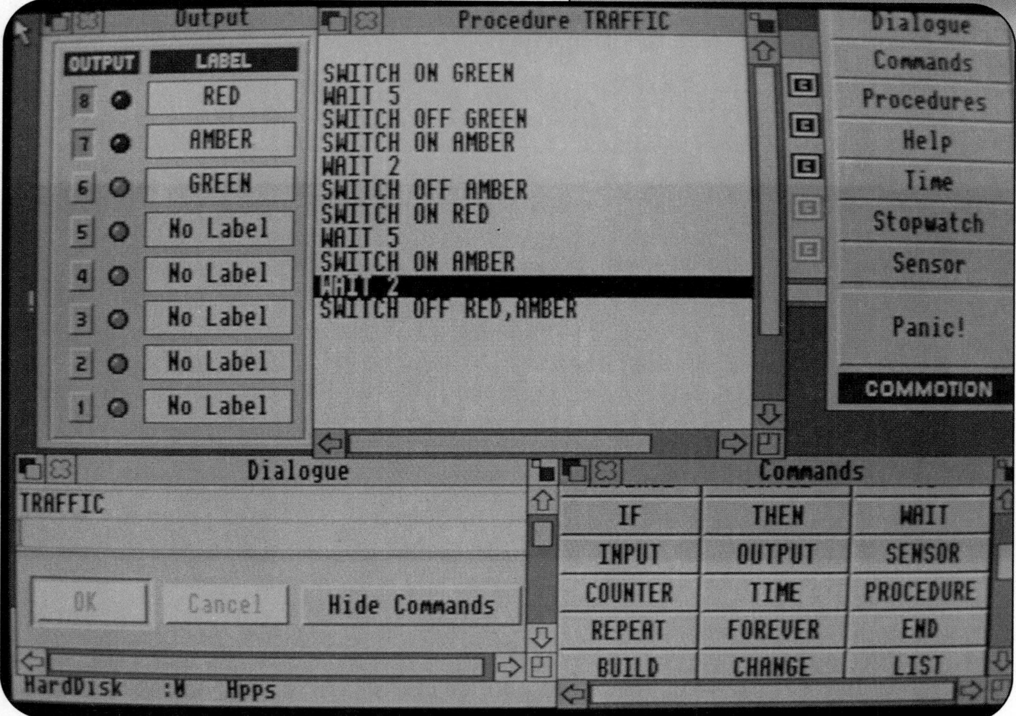

The photograph in Fig. 4.6 shows one possible traffic light sequence, which uses a special control program. The timing of the pauses between the changes has been set to count in tenths of a second in order to speed up the program.

Your lights do not need to be the same as the ones on the interface. Light bulbs can be mounted on a post to simulate a real light system.

◁ **Fig. 4.6 Traffic light program**

DISCO DANCING

If you want to move from the routine world of traffic control to the more exciting world of disco dancing, why not use a simple program to create a lot of different light sequences? You could build a set of coloured lights to represent disco lights. Can they flash rapidly? Can they repeat patterns of light?

Could they be used as lights at your school disco? If not, why not? What would you need to make this possible?

Using electricity from the main socket can be dangerous, so to make a brighter light you might use a larger battery and lights. Car headlights are very bright and can be run from a large car battery. Is it possible to use these high power lights with your interface?

How do you safely find the answer? Consult your teacher.

△ **Fig. 4.7**

MOVE IT!

Controlling movement by computer is more widespread than you might think. Many factories, for example, use robotic machines which are programmed to move components around. Fig. 4.8 shows a moving robot cart transporting a car body shell along an assembly line.

△ **Fig. 4.8**

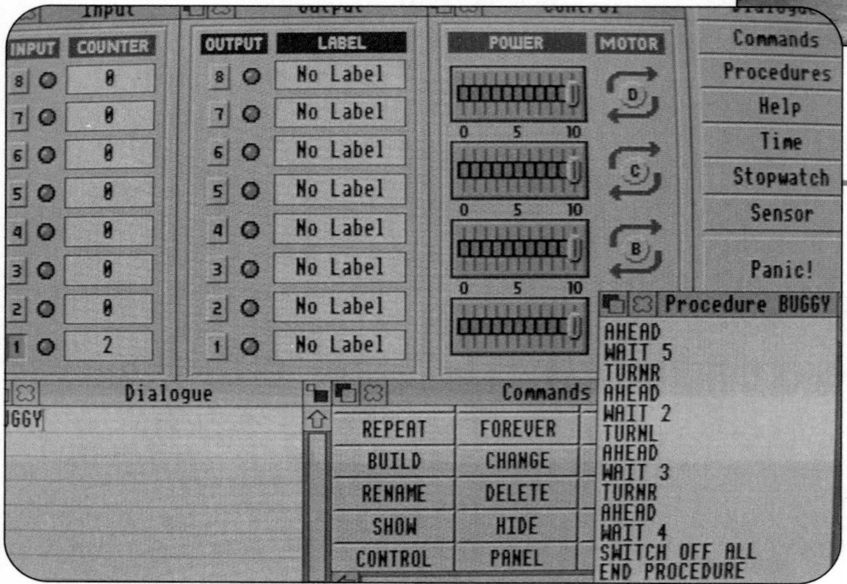

△ **Fig. 4.9 This program controls …**

BUGGIES AND TURTLES

In school, you may have similar devices. They are, of course, much smaller than factory robots, but their movement can be controlled using a computer in just the same way. These devices are called buggies and turtles. Buggies are usually connected to the computer by a cable that transfers the program of instructions from the computer to the device. Turtles, on the other hand, are usually self-contained, with an on-board computer and keyboard. They are given the name 'turtles' because of their curved shell-like covers, sometimes called bodies.

The instructions you use to move your turtle must be short, clear and simple, like those used to control the lights on pages 60 and 61. If the turtle has two motors, each one driving a wheel, it is possible to make it turn an exact number of degrees. Combining these turns with forward or backward movements of specified length allows you to program the turtle to make quite long complicated movements.

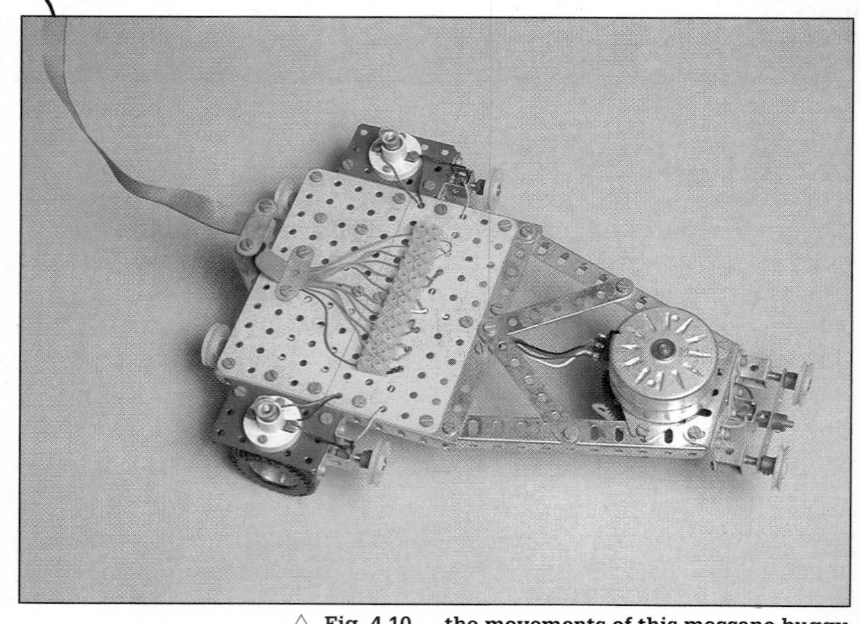

△ **Fig. 4.10 … the movements of this meccano buggy**

When using IT, you will learn:

that programmable devices can be controlled using sequences of instructions

that the order in which instructions are presented, and the form in which they are given to a computer is important

LET'S GO

Try writing a program to make a turtle move from one position to another. To make the task more challenging, put one or two obstructions in the turtle's path. Remember that you will need to program your turtle so that it knows precisely when and how to get round the obstructions: otherwise it will end up having a crash.

Now send your turtle on a return journey. Is it better to move in reverse or to continue going forward after a complete turn around? Does it matter which way you do it? Try them both.

Sample program

1 Move forward 5
2 Stop
3 Turn 90 degrees clockwise
4 Move forward 2
5 Stop
6 Turn 90 degrees anti-clockwise
7 Move forward 4
8 Stop
9 Turn 90 degrees anti-clockwise
10 Move forward 3
11 Stop
12 Turn 90 degrees clockwise
13 Move forward 4
14 Stop

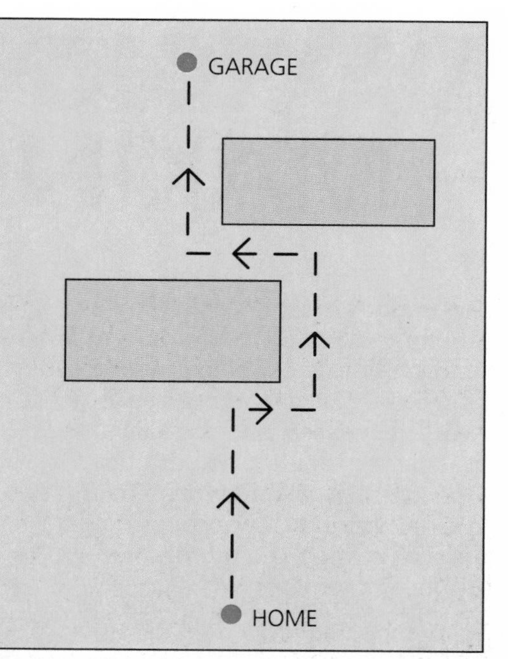

△ **Fig. 4.11**

TRANSFORM YOUR TURTLE

You can customize your turtle to meet your needs by building different bodies to put on to it. With a little imagination you can transform a turtle into anything you want, from an alien spaceship to a fabulous dragon, from a pirate ship to a poodle. When you want to use it for a different purpose, you can simply change your turtle's body.

◁ **Fig. 4.12 Transform your turtle into a high-flying Red Arrow!**

TURTLE TREK

Why not transform your turtle into a spaceship and program it to go where no turtle has been before? You could take over your school hall and create a new solar system by building planets out of junk materials. Arrange the planets in orbit around a huge star. To make the scene more realistic, you might black out the hall by drawing the curtains and decorate the planets and star with luminous paint. Perhaps you could have a light on the front of your spaceship turtle.

When you have built your solar system, send your turtle on a space journey. Program it to move from planet to planet, perhaps in search of a lost cosmonaut, or looking for new forms of life. Instruct it to orbit some of the planets, and then make it dock in a suitable spot. Remember, your turtle cannot think for itself: it can only go where you have programmed it to go.

FORMATION TURTLES

With a team of turtles, perhaps customized as Red Arrow formation flyers or a motorbike display team, you could put on a show of synchronized movement. Take care to program each turtle so that it moves in conjunction with the others and avoids any collisions. If you use buggies for your team display, keep in mind that they have cables attached to them, and make sure that your programs do not leave them in a tangle.

DECISION – MAKING

An important skill for you to develop is the ability to decide whether or not to use Information Technology in your work. Sometimes, it is appropriate to use a word processor, but at other times it is better to use a pen or pencil. For one task you may wish to create a database, but for another it may be that storing the information on paper is adequate, or better.

And once you have decided upon using Information Technology to help you, you may also have an important choice to make between the different tools of Information Technology.

METHODS OF MEASURING

Computers can help you in the control and measurement of scientific experiments. But which Information Technology tools should you use, if any?

The experiment illustrated on this page investigates the insulation properties of different types of cups. Choose a few similar-sized cups made from different materials, such as glass, china, polystyrene or paper, and compare the two methods.

METHOD 1:

- **a** Fill the different cups with equal amounts of water heated to the same temperature.
- **b** Place a thermometer in each cup and note the falling temperature of the water at regular intervals.
- **c** Using a spreadsheet, enter the data and produce an appropriate graph to show the relative cooling curves.
- **d** The cup in which the water remains the hottest for the longest time is the best insulator.

METHOD 2:

- **a** Fill the different cups with equal amounts of water heated to the same temperature.
- **b** Insert sensors into the water and wait while it cools.
- **c** The sensors are connected to a computer which logs the falling temperatures at set intervals. On the computer screen you will see the temperature data displayed as a chart showing the different sensors and their cooling curves.
- **d** The cup in which the water remains the hottest for the longest time is the best insulator.

When using IT, you will learn:

to use Information Technology to work more effectively

that Information Technology is used to monitor physical events and conditions, and to process, present and respond to collected data

COMPARING METHODS

Method 1 involves using a thermometer to measure temperature and a spreadsheet to graph the data. The person following this method has made the decision to use Information Technology on a limited scale. The computer is used to record and analyse the data, but plays no part in collecting the information about the cooling water.

Method 2 uses a computer both to measure and record the temperatures as the sensors respond to the cooling water, as well as to draw the graph. The person following this method has made the decision to use the tools of Information Technology for both stages of the experiment.

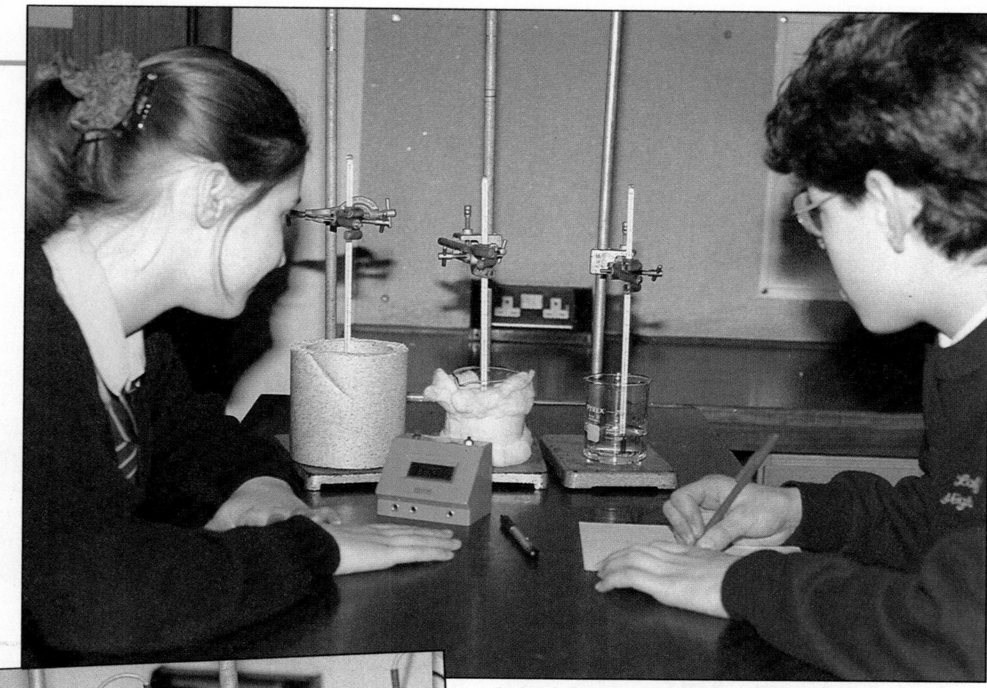

△ **Fig. 4.13 Measuring temperature with a thermometer**

△ **Fig. 4.14 Measuring temperature with sensors**

Compare each stage of the experiment and ask yourself if there are any advantages to each method. Both methods should give the same result: the same cup should be the best insulator. If the results are not exactly the same can you work out why they are different? Which method of measuring temperature should be the more accurate and why?

△ **Fig. 4.15 Sensors in the box on this mast monitor and record wind speed and direction, temperature and rainfall over many days.**

TEMPERATURE CHANGES

Can you think of any other kinds of experiments to measure temperature changes in which the use of sensors would be a more practical and efficient choice than a thermometer?

Think about the difficulties of measuring very high temperatures in an enclosed space. Why might sensors be a good choice in this case?
How might you measure changing temperatures over very short and very long periods of time? Why would the use of a thermometer be difficult in both cases?

Take a breather

Information Technology is not only useful in helping you record the progress of your personal fitness (on a spreadsheet), it can also be used to actually assess your level of fitness. This can be done by using sensors attached to your body.

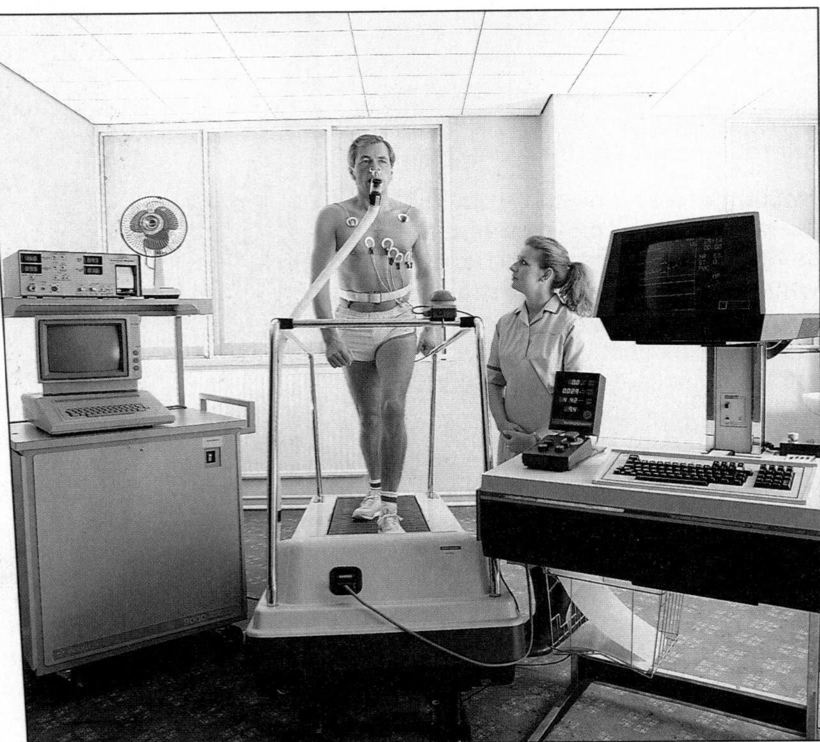

△ **Fig. 4.16 Monitoring heart and lungs**

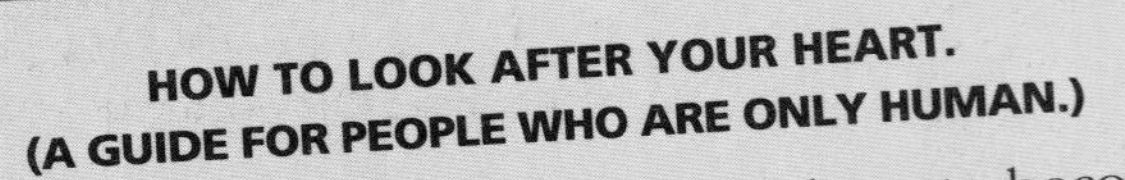

HOW TO LOOK AFTER YOUR HEART.
(A GUIDE FOR PEOPLE WHO ARE ONLY HUMAN.)

Here's some good news. You don't have to become a jogging, teetotal vegetarian to stay young and fit. There are a few easy changes you can make.

MAKE A NEW START

Why be like Andy Capp? Don't forget he is pen and ink but you are flesh and blood.

LOOK AFTER YOUR HEART

When using IT, you will learn:

- *to use Information Technology for investigations requiring the analysis of data*
- *that Information Technology is used to monitor physical events and conditions, and to process, present and respond to collected data*

RECOVERY RATE

Physical fitness is not just measured by how fast you can run 800 metres or by how far you can jump. Another important aspect is the time needed for you to get back to your normal breathing and heart rate after physical exertion – your recovery rate.

There is a close connection between fitness and recovery rate, and there are many things that will affect both, such as smoking, drinking and diet. Anti-smoking campaigns often use adverts showing young people after walking up a flight of stairs, gasping for breath because their heart and lungs have been badly affected by smoking. They obviously need a long time to get their breath back. Compare their recovery rate with that of Olympic athletes who have to run in heats, semi-finals and finals in a short space of time.

Stopwatches or electronic timing are helpful in monitoring fitness as far as speed is concerned. But how might you chart the recovery rate of your heart and lungs?

MEASURE YOUR HEARTBEAT

If your school has sensors which can measure your heart and breathing rates, these can be connected to a computer to enable you to monitor how effective your personal fitness programme has been in improving your recovery rate.

First, measure your heart rate by clipping the sensor, which is connected to the computer, to your ear. It might be a good idea to sit down for a couple of minutes before you attach the sensor as your heart rate may have gone up just by walking quickly to the classroom. Once you have clipped the sensor to your ear, sit for five minutes while the computer maps out a graph of your heart rate on the screen.

Now, remove the sensor and do a set of planned exercises such as sit-ups, squat jumps or press-ups, for five minutes. When you have finished the exercises, attach the sensor once again. The resulting graph will show an increase in your heart rate, which will in time return to normal. How long did it take for your heart rate to return to its normal pattern? Print out the graphs and keep them as part of your fitness profile.

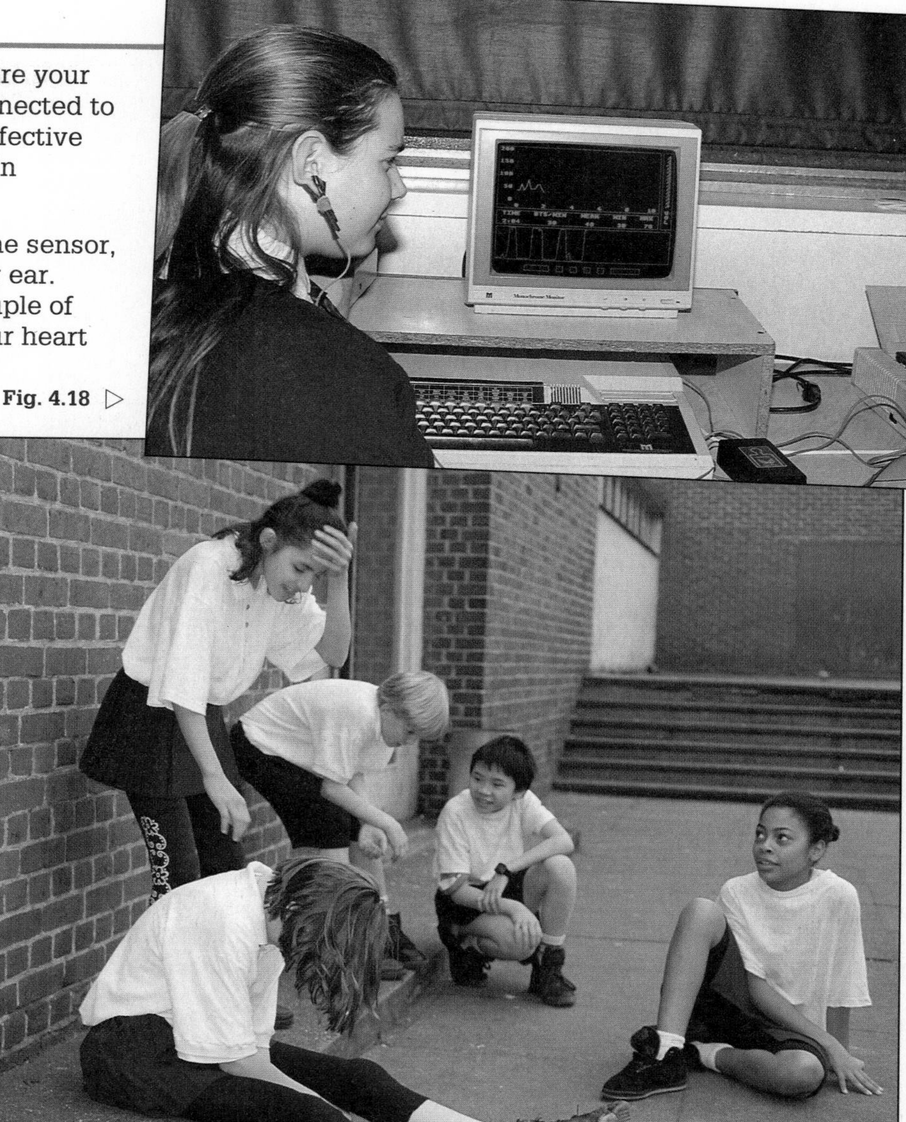

Fig. 4.18 ▷

△ **Fig. 4.19 How quickly do you recover?**

LUNG CAPACITY

A similar kind of process can be carried out using a breath sensor. The computer will receive information about the capacity of your lungs and produce a graph of your performance both before and after exercise. These graphs can be printed out and kept as evidence of the effectiveness of your physical fitness programme.

You will be using methods similar to those used in hospitals, though their equipment is much more sophisticated. Fig. 4.20 shows a hospital's electrocardiograph screen displaying a patient's heart rate.

◁ **Fig. 4.20**

Commercial BREAK

You can use IT to experiment with rhythms and melodies to create new tunes. Try composing a jingle to advertise a well-known product. If your computer has a MIDI interface you can connect it to a keyboard synthesizer, and using an appropriate program, you can take control of your tune.

△ Fig. 4.21

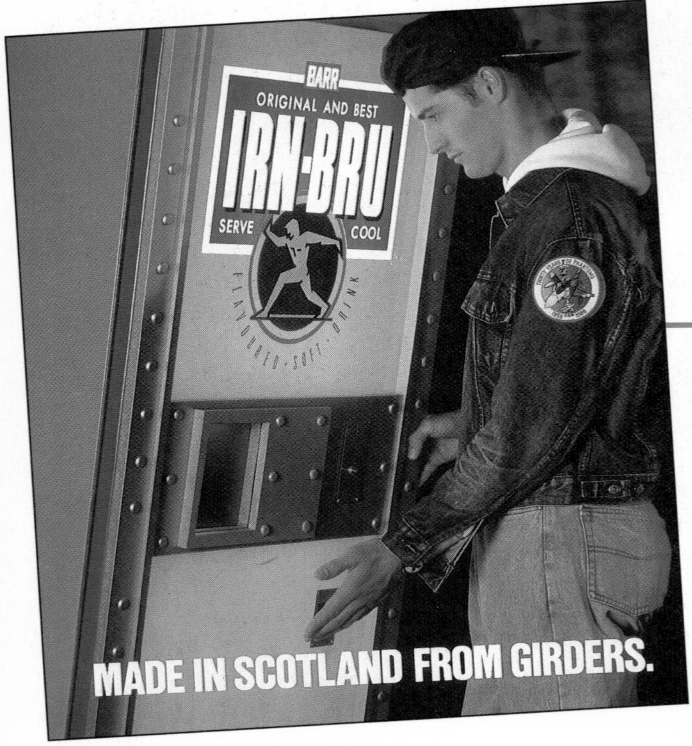

WORDS AND MUSIC

Television adverts must have a strong visual appeal to make an immediate impact. However, it is not just the visual aspect which is important. Both the words and the music which frequently accompany exciting visual images play a vital part in selling the product. Try turning the sound down on your television when the adverts are on: both the words of the actors and the background music are lost, and so is a large part of the impact.

◁ Fig. 4.22

Sometimes the advertiser takes existing pop songs and uses them as background music. However, this does not need a great deal of creative effort, other than matching the song to the product. But to think up a suitable slogan for a particular product and then set that slogan to music does require a good deal of creativity. In performing this task Information Technology can help you to create something original and exciting.

Fig. 4.23 ▷

When using IT, you will learn:

that it is not always necessary to use the computer keyboard in order to produce information

to identify the requirements, and make correct use of Information Technology equipment, software and techniques, in making presentations and reports

CREATE A JINGLE

First, create a memorable slogan to advertise your product. Think of recent successful advertising slogans which you have heard or seen. Think carefully about what makes a successful slogan.

Once you have your slogan, set up your keyboard, software and MIDI interface so that you can begin to experiment with different sounds to go with your slogan.

△ **Fig. 4.24**

You or your group will have to decide on a starting point for the jingle. Perhaps you could play a very simple tune on the keyboard, which consists of a limited range of notes. For example, take a well-known tune, like a nursery rhyme, and play it backwards, perhaps two or three times over. Once you have entered your musical starting point into the computer, you will be able to play it back and adjust it. Is the tempo to your liking? Does the pitch need adjusting at all? Do you need to make some of the musical phrases longer or shorter to fit in with the syllables?

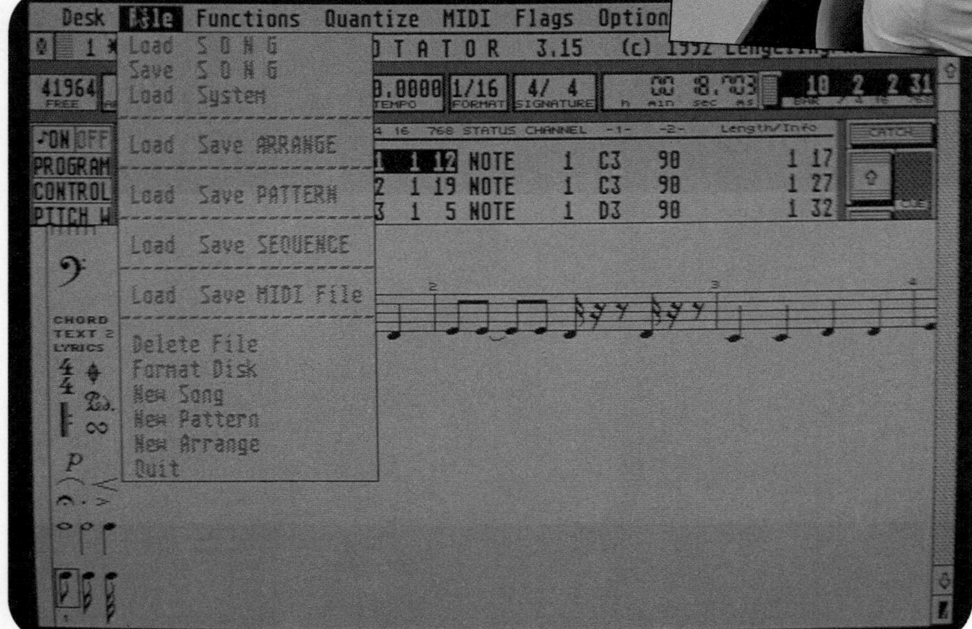

△ **Fig. 4.25 Music programs make it easy to compose**

THE FINAL COMPOSITION

At this point, you may feel that your jingle is finished. On the other hand, you may want to make use of the computer's facilities to build up your simple jingle in order to create something more complex and ambitious. Just as you are able to put together different fonts in a word-processing program to produce a pleasing final piece of work to print out, you can use the computer and its interface to combine different sets of sounds created on the keyboard to produce a final composition. You could print it out as a musical score.

Once you are satisfied that the jingle will sell your product why not sing it in front of the rest of the class, accompanied by your composition. You could also devise a movement or dance routine to go with the jingle and video the final version.

△ **Fig. 4.26 Singing the final jingle**

Gardener's WORLD

If you were asked to name the tools which a gardener uses, what would you say? A spade? A hoe? A lawnmower? A fork? A hose-pipe? Probably. But would you have said a computer? Probably not. However, computer technology can play an important part in the gardener's world.

Fig. 4.27 ▷

IDEAL ENVIRONMENT

Any gardener will tell you that there are four crucial factors which affect the life of a plant:

- Light
- Water
- Food
- Heat

Furthermore, different plants need different amounts of these four variables if they are to flourish. That is why every packet of seeds contains information about the best kind of environment for that particular plant.

However, having all the right information about an ideal environment does not mean that the plant will flourish. The changing weather sometimes means that plants do not get enough water or sunshine. Also, the soil in your garden may not suit the plant; it may, for instance, contain too much lime.

Fig. 4.28 Computer control of nutrients for tomato cultivation △

THE ART OF GARDENING

Clearly, part of the art of gardening is to ensure that plants have the best possible environment. This means trying to control the environment yourself. Watering the garden during an unusually dry period, or pulling out weeds so that flowers do not have to compete for food and light, are very obvious ways of controlling the environment. Using a greenhouse to cultivate plants is another. In the past, using a greenhouse involved a lot of opening and closing of windows to ensure that the temperature inside was neither too high nor too low. Now, large areas of a greenhouse can be controlled by automated computer systems.

When using IT, you will learn:

to write a simple computer program for a particular purpose

MONITORING TEMPERATURE

When used in greenhouses, computers are programmed to monitor the environment by measuring continually such things as inside and outside temperatures, and the amount of moisture in the soil and in the air.

The computer is programmed to respond to specific readings or levels. At night, for example, when the temperature falls below a certain level, the heating system in the greenhouse is switched on. During sunny days, if the temperature rises above the desired maximum then ventilation is used – the computer opens windows to allow heat to escape. If the temperature outside is too high for this to have an effect, then the windows are closed and cool air is circulated.

To make it fully automatic the system includes what is known as a 'feedback loop'.

WHAT IS A FEEDBACK LOOP?

A feedback loop uses continuous monitoring to control a system. Your body has many very efficient feedback loops. You are continually monitoring lots of different things. Try standing on one leg: you will soon start to wobble. When this happens the balance sensors in your ears send a message to your brain, so that the wobble can be corrected. Once corrected, your balance sensors tell your brain that all is well. If the feedback loop in your system is not efficient you will fall over.

In the case of the greenhouse, the computer constantly monitors the various levels, and adjusts its instructions accordingly.

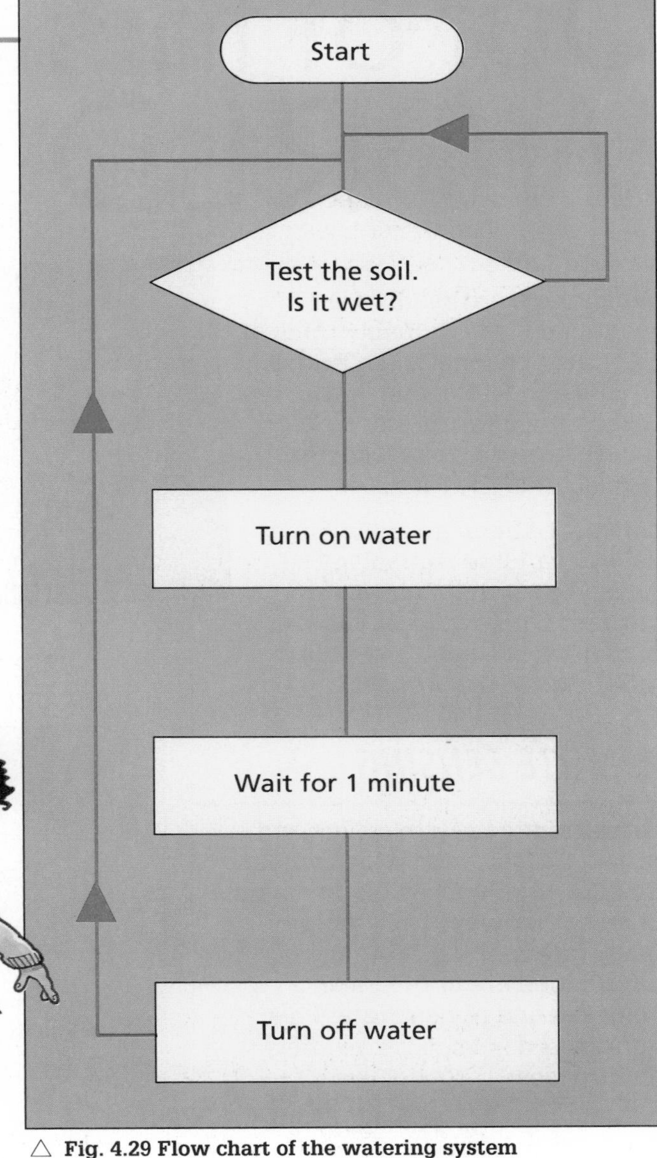

△ **Fig. 4.29 Flow chart of the watering system**

Fig. 4.30

PLANT-CARE CHALLENGE

During school holidays your school plants are no longer under your care. How might you make sure they receive regular watering without asking the caretaker to help? Is it possible to use a computer system to create an environment in which they can continue to flourish?

Your challenge is to devise a simple computer program for an automatic watering system using electrically operated taps to control water flow. It is quite easy to obtain the taps – ask your teacher.

Use moisture sensors to monitor the water content of the soil. If your school has a lot of plants in separate pots, rather than monitoring and watering each one separately, you could place a few pots on a tray of sand. That way you would be able to monitor and water the sand to keep the plants' soil moist.

To help you, why not visit your nearest garden centre or nursery to see how computer systems help them to maintain their plants.

Out of this WORLD

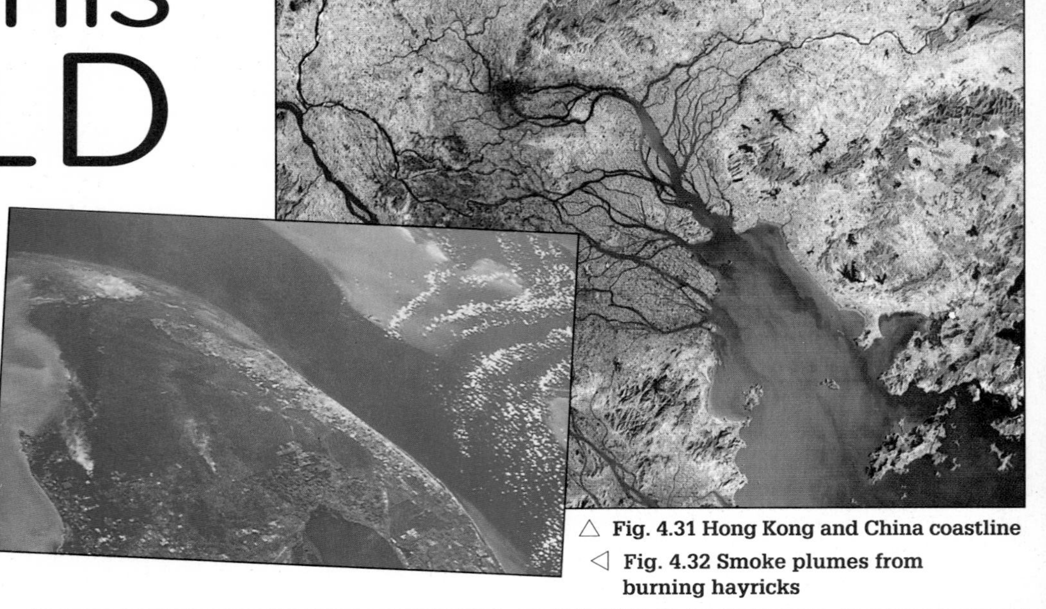

△ Fig. 4.31 Hong Kong and China coastline

◁ Fig. 4.32 Smoke plumes from burning hayricks

When the word satellite is mentioned, you probably think of television channels, like British Sky Broadcasting, and of the dishes stuck on the sides of houses in order to receive the signals from the satellite.

However, there are many more uses of satellite technology beyond providing television viewers with a greater variety of films or live sport from the other side of the world.

REMOTE SENSING

Satellites are used to collect and provide information which would be difficult or impossible to obtain in any other way. They gather many different kinds of information about the Earth's land, sea and atmosphere. This information is used for a variety of purposes:

- to study land and sea formations (as in Fig. 4.31)
- to forecast the weather
- to record and analyse pollution (as in Fig. 4.32)
- to monitor the activities of other countries

This use of technology to make observations from a distance and produce information from them is called remote sensing.

REMOTE SENSING SYSTEM

INPUT

STAGE 1 is the collection of information.

In remote sensing this is achieved by collecting the different rays coming from the Earth's surface or from the atmosphere above it. There are two main types of rays which are collected:

- visible light rays
- infra-red rays

Visible rays are the rays which we would be able to see looking down to Earth from space. Infra-red rays are invisible rays emitted from objects. The strength of infra-red rays varies according to the temperature of the object.

PROCESSING

STAGE 2 is the processing of collected information by the computer.

The satellite images are translated into code which can be transmitted to dish receivers on the Earth's surface. These are rather like the British Sky Broadcasting dishes, but larger.

The information is collected at the receiving station's computer for analysis.

OUTPUT

STAGE 3 is the output of stored and analysed information.

Different users of the systems require different forms of information. Map-makers, for example, require precise information to scale, so that they can take measurements. Weather forecasters, on the other hand, require details about cloud covering and atmosphere, rather than about land. They need a series of images in order to detect changing patterns of weather.

When using IT, you will learn:

that Information Technology is used to monitor physical events and conditions, and to process, present and respond to collected data

WHAT ARE SATELLITES?

Satellites are man-made objects which are projected into space and travel at high speed in orbit above the Earth. Some satellites travel 30,000 kilometres up over the Equator at the 'same speed' as the Earth. (They travel one complete orbit in exactly one day.) Because of this they remain at the same point above Earth, and it appears that they are stationary in the sky, which is why they are called geostationary satellites. They have small rockets fitted to them so that their position can be adjusted when necessary. When the fuel for the rocket is eventually used up, the satellite will slow down and fall from its orbit, burning up on re-entry into the Earth's atmosphere.

Other satellites follow a polar orbit, which at approximately 600–1500 km above the Earth, is much lower than that of the geostationary satellites. In a polar orbit the satellite moves through a series of North–South paths close to the poles and gradually passes over every part of the Earth to collect information.

△ **Fig. 4.33**

There are well over 2500 satellites in orbit as you are reading this book. You may have heard of some of the following satellites:

Landsat

The Landsat satellites are in polar orbit around the Earth and have been in operation since 1972. They transmit meteorological and environmental information from infra-red and visible light sensors.

Meteosat

The first European Meteosat geostationary satellites were launched in 1977. Now, Meteosat 4 satellites are in orbit sending visible light and infra-red information about cloud movement, the surface temperatures of the sea and land, atmospheric temperatures, and so on. This information is transmitted throughout the day.

NOAA

The NOAA satellites, like Landsat, circle the Earth in a polar orbit. NOAA stands for National Oceanic and Atmospheric Administration. These satellites send meteorological information back to ground stations on Earth.

ACCURATE PREDICTIONS

Information gathered from the remote sensors of the different satellites, as well as from weather ships and balloons, is transmitted and gathered at ground stations. The interpretation of this information helps meteorologists to predict the weather more accurately. So next time you switch on the television or look at teletext to check the weather for the next few days, think how much Information Technology has helped to give you reliable predictions about sunshine, wind and rain.

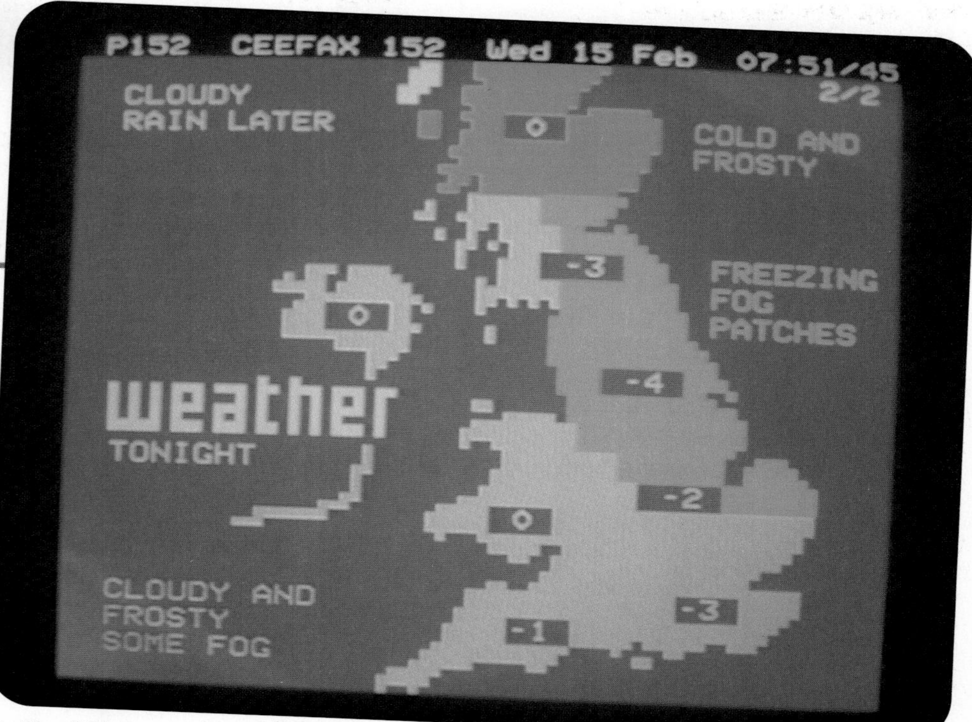

△ **Fig. 4.34**

SPORTS DAY WEATHER PERMITTING

If your class were given the task of forecasting the weather for a school sports day or for a school walk, how would you do it? It would, of course, depend upon what information sources were available to you.

You could listen to the television weather forecast or check the weather charts in the newspapers. But that way, you would only find out what the weather was going to be the day before the event. If you discovered that there was going to be heavy rain, there would be very little time to prepare for it. The organizers would want accurate weather predictions well in advance of the event to give them time to plan.

△ **Fig. 4.35 Collecting data from a Stevenson screen**

△ **Fig. 4.36**

It is essential that all the different types of data are carefully observed and analysed. It is possible to predict the approach of clouds, but it is not so easy to predict whether rain will fall or not. It would be a pity if on Sports Day the refreshment tent collapsed because of an unexpected torrential downpour!

WEATHER PATTERNS

If your school has its own weather station, you would analyse the data it collects on maximum and minimum temperature, precipitation, wind direction and speed, cloud type, and so on, over a period of time. Employing these methods, you might also use Information Technology to help you in the analysis of weather patterns by using a spreadsheet to record and graph the data.

You could also use Information Technology to detect weather patterns if your school has a receiving system to collect data from a satellite such as Meteosat 4 (see Figs 4.36 and 4.37). It would then be possible to compare your local records of day to day changes in the weather with the satellite images downloaded over the same period of time. You would then be in a position to give a reasonably accurate forecast, based upon a variety of data sources.

When using IT, you will learn:

that Information Technology is used to monitor physical events and conditions, and to process, present and respond to collected data

to integrate more than one form of information into a single presentation or report for a particular audience

WEATHER PRESENTATION

As you would have put a good deal of effort into collecting and analysing your information, why not do more with it than just predicting the weather?

There will be many pupils in your school, probably younger than you, who know absolutely nothing about how weather data is collected and analysed. You might do a presentation for these pupils using data gathered from a variety of sources, including your remote sensing system. During the course of your presentation you might demonstrate the various skills necessary to interpret statistics collected from the weather station and from the images downloaded from the satellite.

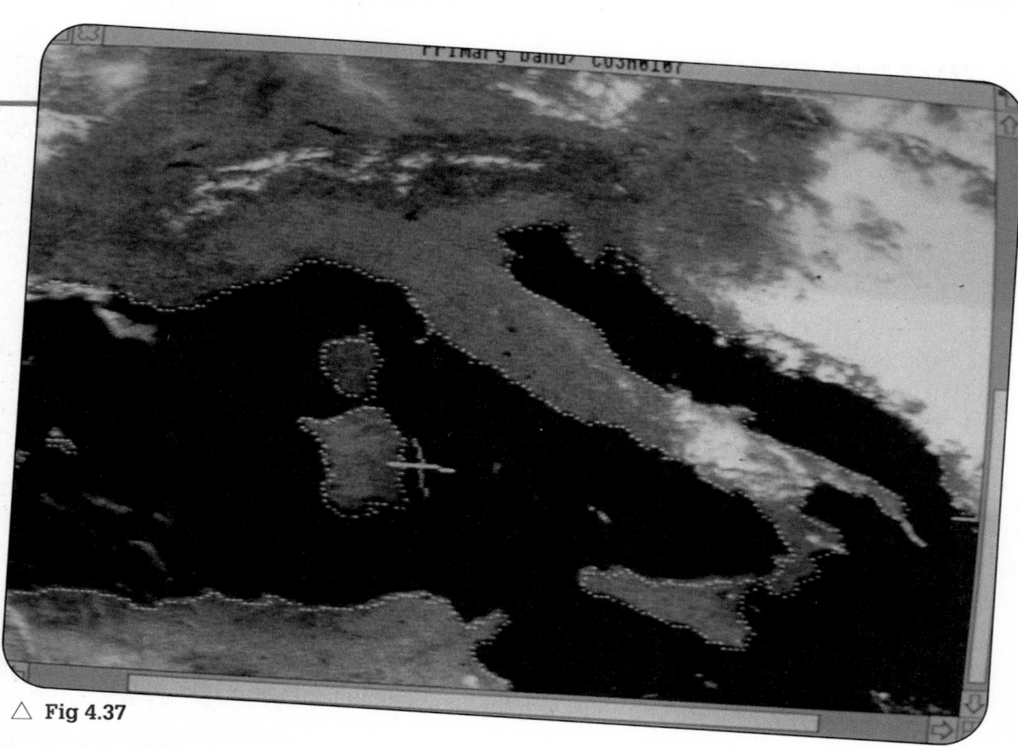

△ Fig 4.37

△ Fig 4.38

WEATHER DISPLAY

Alternatively, you might mount a display of the different kinds of weather data, with a word-processed explanation about the sources of information. How easy or difficult was it to collect and analyse the information? Were the satellite images more reliable than the statistics from the ground weather station? Did Information Technology make the work of collection and analysis easier?

Finally, you might act out the role of the television forecaster, presenting weather charts in relation to a series of printed satellite images which show changing weather conditions over an area of Britain.

△ Fig 4.39

5 APPLICATIONS AND EFFECTS

IT IDEAS FOR EACH SUBJECT

English	◆ Dramatize the sales talk of someone trying to sell various pieces of software **see page 86**. ◇ Identify and discuss the advantages and disadvantages of using a word processor for drafting.
Maths	◆ Map out those places in a local town which use IT to handle statistical information **see page 77**. ◇ Discuss the advantages and disadvantages of using electronic calculators.
Science	◇ Produce a booklet for Year 7 pupils explaining how specific pieces of software can help them in their work. ◇ Consider the way in which satellite technology raises awareness of global environmental problems.
Technology	◆ Discuss the problem of inappropriate and irresponsible use of IT **see page 88**. ◇ Consider the usefulness of the information sources used in the development of a design proposal.
Modern Languages	◇ Compare a foreign exchange visit with an interactive video simulation as a learning experience. ◇ Produce a booklet for Year 7 pupils suggesting how they might make use of the school's audio and video equipment in independent activities.
Geography	◆ Plan a journey using IT and without using IT: compare the processes **see page 78**. ◇ Discuss margins of error in weather forecasting techniques.
History	◇ Compare the experience of a historical simulation with reading about the event in a textbook. ◆ Compare the de-skilling of workers by the IT revolution with parallel examples from the past **see page 84**.
Art	◇ Make a User Guide to explain possible applications of the graphics programs in the school software library. ◇ Discuss the impact of the computer on the evolution of artistic activity.
Music	◇ Dramatize an argument between two pupils, one of whom has benefited from using IT in Music and one of whom disapproves of using IT. ◇ Consider the impact of computer-generated sound on popular music.
PE	◇ Discuss how the facilities of the video camera can help to improve a dancer's performance. ◇ Compare the experience of live sport with that of a simulated game, both as a participant and a spectator.
RE/PSE	◆ Discuss the ethical problems surrounding the holding of computerized information by the state and its institutions **see page 82**. ◇ Consider the impact of computers or arcade games upon the quality of family relationships.
Economic & Industrial Understanding	◆ Examine the impact of IT on a working environment such as a public library **see page 80**. ◇ Discuss the concept of tele-shopping as part of the changing patterns of consumerism.
Careers	◇ Interview the school careers officer to find out the importance of computer literacy in the job market. ◇ Visit a local company which makes extensive use of IT.
Health	◇ Consider IT as an administrative tool in the service of the NHS. ◇ Visit a local health centre to investigate the use of IT for health care.
Citizenship	◆ Consider IT in terms of equal opportunities for people with disabilities **see page 90**. ◆ Evaluate the impact of possible overuse of electronic games as a leisure activity **see page 88**.
Environmental Education	◇ Identify the impact of computer technology on a specific community. ◇ Consider the strengths and weaknesses of evidence based upon computer model projections in a debate on an environmental issue.

Here, there and everywhere

Information Technology is all around us. There is no escape. You only have to take a walk down any High Street of any town or city to see Information Technology in action.

Look at this map of an imaginary High Street. It shows where the skills which you are learning in school are also being used in everyday life. People shopping and working in the High Street are using the tools of Information Technology to handle and communicate information, in the same way as you use them in the classroom.

If you live in or near a town or city, you might like to make your own IT map to chart the places where IT is being used and for what purposes. You can include offices, shops, public buildings and transport.

Once you have mapped out the areas of a town or city in which IT is employed, you could think about what methods of working have been replaced by this new technology. What advantages have been gained by using IT? Are there any disadvantages?

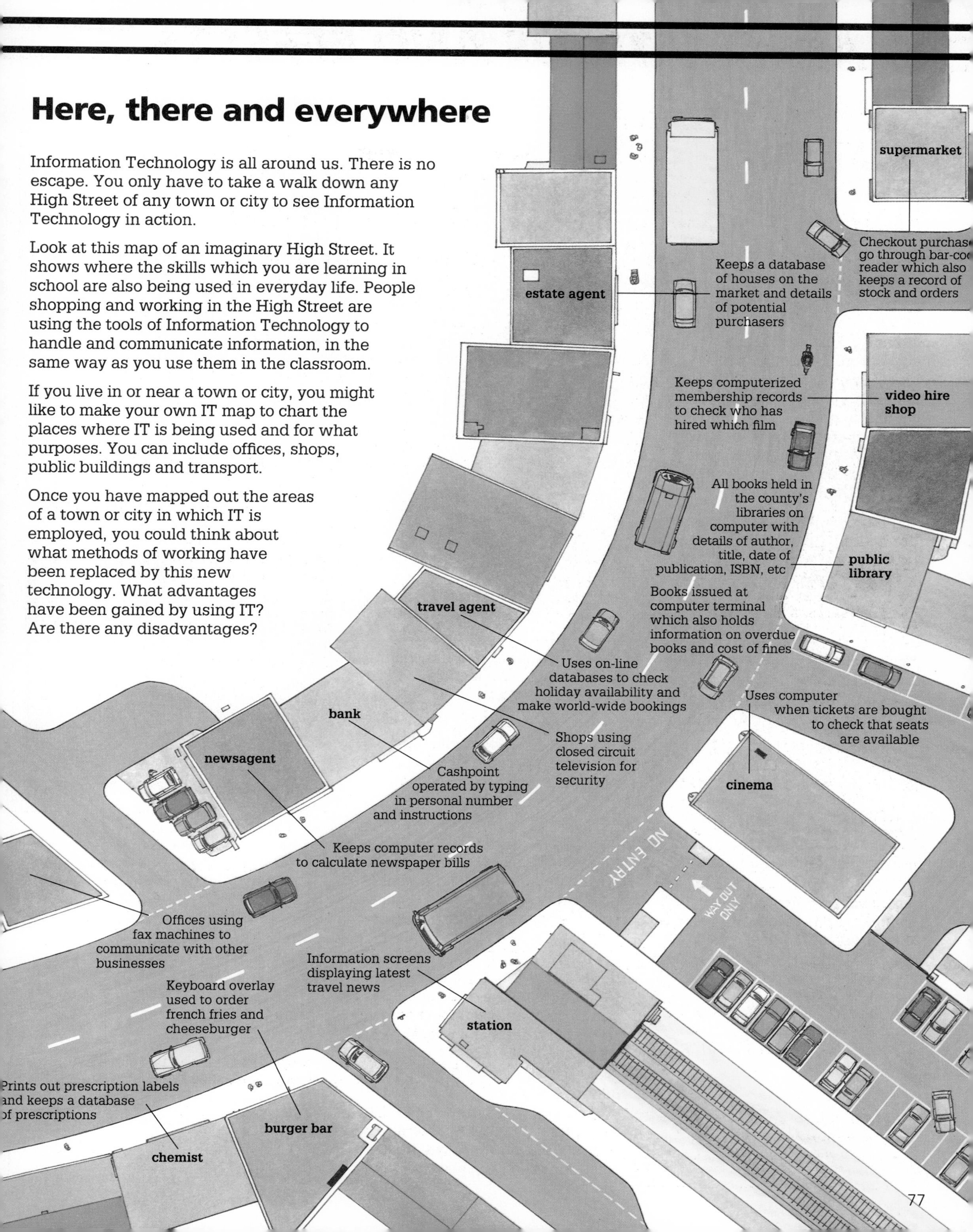

We're all going on a SUMMER HOLIDAY

Packing your own suitcase is one of the many preparations which have to be made before going on holiday. In order to pack effectively, you have to plan ahead and consider what you'll need at your holiday destination. For parents, however, there is more to do than simply pack suitcases. Between deciding to go on holiday and actually arriving at the destination, there is a great deal of planning and organizing to be done, without which the holiday could be disastrous.

Planning a holiday takes time, but Information Technology has helped to make the organization more convenient and efficient.

PLANNING A HOLIDAY

How would *you* go about planning a holiday and what use would you make of Information Technology? Below you will find some suggestions. Read them through and then make your own holiday plans.

The first stage, obviously, is deciding where to go. Most people like to browse through holiday brochures to get some ideas before making a booking. However, before making any decision, you might flick through the holiday pages on teletext (Fig. 5.1) to check for any special offers.

P300 ORACLE 300 Tue13 Nov ITV 1705:50

WEATHER TRAVEL + HOLIDAY GUIDE

Weather Guide	301
Travel Reports	310
British Airways Arrivals	321
Holiday News	340
Holiday Ads:	350
Overseas Holidays	351
Just Flights	360
UK Holidays	380

Main Index 100 Your Region 200

KAYS AUTUMN/WINTER SAVERS page 193

△ Fig. 5.1

BOOKING A HOLIDAY

If you are using the services of a travel agent, you will see immediately how Information Technology has made the organization of holidays easier. Every travel agent now has a range of computer terminals giving access to huge databases. These will give you all the information necessary to book your holiday, as well as allowing your travel agent to key into the database all the relevant information about you and your family. Your travel agent will have a computer terminal which gives rapid access to airline companies all over the world, so that you can book your flights there and then. When you reserve a seat on a flight your details are instantly recorded in the airline's computers, which may be 10,000 miles away, so that no one else can book that seat. There will be a terminal which has access to the databases of tour companies, so that the availability of travel tickets on the dates you require, and rooms at the hotel which you have chosen, can be checked. All this information is up-to-date and reliable. Your travel agent will probably have a word processor too, for day-to-day administration, such as accounts, receipts and letters.

How were holidays booked before the development of the computer? Compare the time needed to book a holiday thirty years ago with the swift, simple procedure of today.

When using IT, you will learn:

to use IT for investigations requiring the analysis of data

to review and discuss your use of IT applications and to consider related applications in the outside world, and their impact on daily life

PLANNING THE ROUTE

Once your holiday has been booked, you may want to use other aspects of Information Technology to organize the journey. If you are travelling by car to an airport or to your destination, you will need to plan the best route. You might use a road atlas; on the other hand, some portable computers have route planners which do all the hard work for you, not only planning the journey, but also calculating the number of miles to be travelled (see Fig. 5.3). If you are travelling by train, you could check your route and any connections using paper timetables or by queuing up at the enquiry desk. However, you may be able to use computerized journey planners which some stations now have. Alternatively, if you have access to British Rail's on-line database you could use the information found there to plan the early stages of the journey.

These are just a few examples of how Information Technology might help you to plan and organize a holiday efficiently. But, unfortunately, a computer cannot help you to pack your suitcase!

△ **Fig. 5.2 World-wide information at her fingertips**

Fig. 5.3 Different ways of planning a journey

New-Look LIBRARIES

Public libraries in this country have changed almost beyond recognition over the last thirty years. And the change has been for the good.

LIBRARIES OF THE PAST

In the past, public libraries often had rather an unattractive image. The atmosphere was sometimes very unfriendly, especially for children. The rule of strict silence was enforced and any conversations had to be in whispers. Finding a book was a real challenge. Details of all the books were filed on thousands of index cards, often handwritten, and these were packed tightly into drawers. Borrowing or returning a book was also tedious and time-consuming. Each book had its own ticket which had to be filed away with the borrower's details every time the book was loaned. This ticket then had to be found and replaced when the book was returned.

In short, going to the library was not always an enjoyable experience because the library was not user-friendly.

△ **Fig. 5.4 An old-fashioned library**

LIBRARIES NOW

How did the public library become more user-friendly? Putting carpet down on the floor and using bookshelves which children could reach certainly helped. More significant was the idea that a library wasn't just a warehouse for books, and that it should appeal to a greater range of people. The library came to be seen as a place where information of all kinds might be made available to the people in the community. Just look in your local library to see what is there. You will probably find records and CDs for loan, pictures and posters, newspapers and local directories, as well as an excellent range of books and magazines.

Most important of all, the use of Information Technology means that borrowers can get information more quickly and the librarians can do their jobs more efficiently. Instead of a filing system, libraries now keep records of all their books on a computer database. The librarian can now tell you in a matter of seconds whether or not the library has a particular book and, if so, whether it has been borrowed or is still on the shelves. If the computer system is networked with other libraries in the area, the librarian can also check to see if the book can be found in a library nearby.

When using IT, you will learn:

that IT can be used to do things which can also be done in other ways

that computers are used to store personal information

THE SPEED OF LIGHT

It has become much quicker to issue a book too, since the librarian can record the process simply by running a light pen (Fig. 5.5) over the bar code on the borrower's library card, or by using a laser bar-code scanner (Fig. 5.6). This automatically transfers the necessary details into the computer.

Many bookshops now have similar systems, so that they too can tell you exactly what they have in stock. When you buy a book, the sales assistant runs the light pen across the book's bar code and the price is registered on the till. This process avoids mistakes which could occur when keying in the price manually. It's also much quicker and, because it records everything that is bought from the shop, it is very useful for keeping track of stock levels.

△ Fig. 5.5

◁ Fig. 5.6

Why not pay a visit to your local library and observe these IT innovations for yourself? Make a note of the following:

- How quickly can the librarian issue and discharge books using a light pen and the bar code on the book?
- How can the librarian check if a book is available in any other of the libraries in the area?
- How quickly can the librarian make a list of available books by the same author without looking on the shelves?
- What other kinds of electronic information are available (for example, teletext and CD-ROMs)?

In what other ways is your library user-friendly? Might it make further improvements using IT?

◁ **Fig. 5.7 A modern library**

False information . . .	can damage your HEALTH

The world is full of information which is increasing every second of every day and will never run out. Every day we all produce, process and consume vast quantities of it. Details are passed from one person to another who passes them on to someone else. It is not surprising, therefore, that misunderstandings and mistakes sometimes occur. But, unfortunately, what begins as a tiny error can end up as a huge disaster for someone.

WE ARE ALL ON FILE

Large quantities of information are stored away in computers, including information which relates to all of us. Take a look at the Vehicle Registration Document in Fig. 5.8, which every car owner must have. The document contains information relating to the car and the people who have owned the car. All this information about every single vehicle on our roads is held on a computer at the Driver Vehicle Licence Centre (DVLC) in Swansea. Imagine the time and effort saved by using computers at the DVLC and in other organizations which use technology to store their information.

It is important that information is completely up-to-date and accurate in order to protect individual citizens. Sometimes people entering information into computers make mistakes. If information about a person held on a computer is wrong or out of date, it could have serious results for that person. They might end up losing their jobs or even being arrested. For instance, if someone is driving a car that is not registered in their name on the DVLC computer, the police might think that they have stolen it! That is why if any of the details on the Vehicle Registration Document change, the car owner must inform the DVLC immediately.

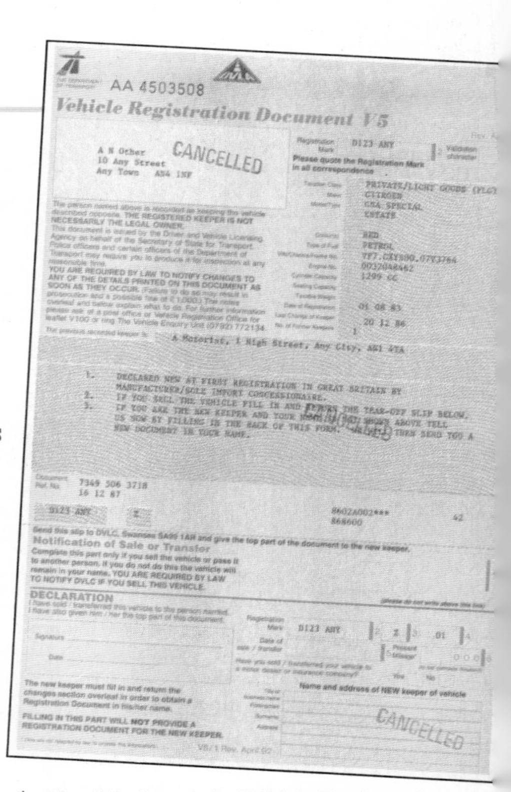
AA 4503508

Vehicle Registration Document V5

A N Other
10 Any Street
Any Town AN4 1NF

CANCELLED

Registration Mark: D123 ANY

Please quote the Registration Mark in all correspondence

PRIVATE/LIGHT GOODS (PLG)
CITROEN
GSA SPECIAL
ESTATE

RED
PETROL
1299 CC

01 08 83
20 12 86
1

The person named above is recorded as keeping the vehicle described opposite. THE REGISTERED KEEPER IS NOT NECESSARILY THE LEGAL OWNER.

YOU ARE REQUIRED BY LAW TO NOTIFY CHANGES TO ANY OF THE DETAILS PRINTED ON THIS DOCUMENT AS SOON AS THEY OCCUR.

A Motorist, 1 High Street, Any City, AN1 4TA

1. DECLARED NEW AT FIRST REGISTRATION IN GREAT BRITAIN BY MANUFACTURER/SOLE IMPORT CONCESSIONAIRE.
2. IF YOU SELL THE VEHICLE FILL IN AND RETURN THE TEAR-OFF SLIP BELOW.
3. IF YOU ARE THE NEW KEEPER AND YOUR NAME IS NOT SHOWN ABOVE TELL US NOW BY FILLING IN THE BACK OF THIS FORM. WE WILL THEN SEND YOU A NEW DOCUMENT IN YOUR NAME.

Document Ref. No. 7349 506 3718
16 12 87

D123 ANY

Send this slip to DVLC, Swansea SA99 1AR and give the top part of the document to the new keeper.

Notification of Sale or Transfer

Complete this part only if you sell the vehicle or pass it to another person. If you do not do this the vehicle will remain in your name. YOU ARE REQUIRED BY LAW TO NOTIFY DVLC IF YOU SELL THIS VEHICLE.

DECLARATION

Signature

Date

Registration Mark D123 ANY

Date of sale / transfer

Name and address of NEW keeper of vehicle

The new keeper must fill in and return the changes section overleaf in order to obtain a Registration Document in his/her name.

FILLING IN THIS PART WILL NOT PROVIDE A REGISTRATION DOCUMENT FOR THE NEW KEEPER.

CANCELLED

△ **Fig. 5.8 A sample Vehicle Registration Document**

When using IT, you will learn:
that outcomes are affected by incorrect data, inappropriate procedures, limitations in the methods of data capture and the techniques of enquiry used to retrieve information
that computers are used to store personal information

ELIZABETH II

Data Protection Act 1984

1984 CHAPTER 35

An Act to regulate the use of automatically processed information relating to individuals and the provision of services in respect of such information.
[12th July 1984]

BE IT ENACTED by the Queen's most Excellent Majesty, by and with the advice and consent of the Lords Spiritual and Temporal, and Commons, in this present Parliament assembled, and by the authority of the same, as follows:—

PART I

PRELIMINARY

1.—(1) The following provisions shall have effect for the interpretation of this Act.

Definition of "data" and related expressions.

(2) "Data" means information recorded in a form in which it can be processed by equipment operating automatically in response to instructions given for that purpose.

(3) "Personal data" means data consisting of information which relates to a living individual who can be identified from that information (or from that and other information in the possession of the data user), including any expression of opinion about the individual but not any indication of the intentions of the data user in respect of that individual.

(4) "Data subject" means an individual who is the subject of personal data.

A 2

△ **Fig. 5.9**

CREDIT INFORMATION

There are companies called credit reference agencies that keep database records of people who have taken out loans and who use credit cards. When shoppers want to buy goods on credit or hire purchase, stores can run credit searches with these agencies to establish whether or not the customer will eventually be able to pay for the goods. Before agreeing to let the customer buy on credit, the shop asks the agency for a 'rating' of that customer. If the customer has previously failed to repay a loan or is heavily in debt to a credit card company he or she will have been 'blacklisted' with the agency. The agency will then pass on this information to the shop and the customer will be refused a loan. Occasionally, however, a shop will receive false information, perhaps because the customer has the same name as a blacklisted person, and will deny the customer credit. If this happens, something has clearly gone wrong with the system. Someone, somewhere, is holding information which is wrong or out of date.

DATA PROTECTION ACT

To try and ensure that information about individuals held on computer databases is accurate, the Data Protection Act (Fig. 5.9) was introduced in 1984. This Act gave all of us the right to know what information is held about us and the right to correct that information if it is wrong.

The Data Protection Act is essential to safeguard the freedom of the individual who becomes a victim of wrong information.

Grandmother shocked by gigantic electricity bill

The electricity board was forced to apologise yesterday after sending out a bill for a colossal £4,000,000. They have spent the whole day examining their records to see how such a huge mistake was made. It seems th
noughts

Would you credit it?

A judge today condemned credit reference agencies for not being vigilant enough after Timothy Richards (24) of South Shields was convicted of 8

He had managed to get credit and loans totalling £729,000 by using false names
addresses

Treated like a criminal!

s M J Evans (43) of Cork Street, West ton, was shocked and insulted today er being refused credit in the kitchen partment of her local Blackwell's store, here she has been doing her shopping r over 20 years.

Daughter's Defence

he had been meaning to get a new asher-drier for a couple of months', said aughter Amanda (21). 'And had decided at she could afford to get it on HP. She always very careful with money and I now she would have paid back the loan.'

Blacklisted

Mrs Evans had asked for a loan of £300 after putting down a deposit of £50 on a £350 washer-drier. After she had filled in a detailed form, Blackwell's had followed their normal procedure of having a credit search done on Mrs Evans. The credit reference agency used by Blackwell's found out that Mrs Evans's name was blacklisted and she was refused credit. Their computer showed that she had defaulted on a bank loan for a car and that she was behind with her mortgage repayments.

Computers Never Lie

'It's completely untrue', said Amanda. 'She's never owed money in her life and they treated her like a criminal!'

A spokesperson for Blackwell's only comment was, 'Computers never lie.'

NEWSPAPER REPORTING

It is not unusual to read stories in the newspapers about people receiving bills for astonishing amounts of money that they didn't spend. In groups you might like to write a newspaper article which reports a similar story. You would, of course, have to work out how this kind of mistaken information got into the computer, as well as predicting how someone in this situation is likely to have felt and what excuses might have been offered to explain the situation. You might follow this up by dramatizing a sequel to the newspaper report. How might it have turned out? How easy would it have been to correct the information?

You would find it hard to imagine a world without computers. They are as much a part of everyday life for you as record players were for your parents when they were young. You will have used computers in primary school, you will certainly use them in secondary school and you may have a computer at home. For you, the computer revolution holds no fears: computers are useful, and computers are fun.

△ **Fig. 5.10 Down with machinery!**

When using IT, you will learn:

That IT can be used to do things which can also be done in other ways

THE THREAT OF IT

However, people older than you have had to get used to computers. For some people the new technology of computers was frightening, simply because it *was* new and different and they didn't understand it.

Some people were afraid of computer technology because it threatened their jobs. Computerized machinery was introduced into factories in order to make production more efficient. At the same time, it meant that some people were replaced by machines and found themselves out of a job. Other people were suddenly forced to learn how to use computer technology at work.

FEAR OF CHANGE

This fear of new technology is not unique. In the last century, new machinery in the factories meant more efficient production, but it also meant that old skills were no longer required. Jobs were lost and old ways of working were abandoned. The new technology caused resentment and despair. In some cases, the fear and anger led to violence and resulted in gangs smashing the hated new machines (as in Fig. 5.10). These gangs of technology wreckers were called Luddites.

COMPUTERS IN SCHOOLS

In every job where computers have come on the scene there is some suspicion and fear. Your own school is no exception. Ten years ago very few computers were available in schools. Now it is not unusual for subject departments to have their own computers, as well as access to a Resource Centre. Many teachers, like the one in Fig. 5.11, are at home with computers in the class, but some teachers, especially those who have been working for many years without the help of computers, are very wary of the new technology.

△ **Fig. 5.11**

THE NEO-LUDDITES' REVENGE

Imagine coming into school one morning to find that all the computers, monitors, disk drives and printers have been sent to a car-boot sale, along with all the school's software. A note has been left claiming that this is the work of the Neo-Luddites, a gang of teachers dedicated to wiping out any sign of Information Technology in school and determined to return to pre-computer methods of teaching and learning.

They have also left a series of demands, listed on the blackboard below. Using the only computer which escaped the attention of the teachers, how would you reply to the ideas of the Neo-Luddites? You will be looking at the use of the computer in the classroom from your point of view, but you might like to list the benefits which the teachers might gain from using computers in their lessons. Or you could consider examples in the outside world and examine the good and bad effects of IT. Do the Neo-Luddites have any valid opinions with which you agree?

A nice little earner

△ **Fig. 5.12**

Could you sell software? You may not think you know enough about it, but during your time at school you will have had the opportunity to use a variety of software packages in different lessons. The more you have used the school's software, the more familiar you will have become with what it can and can't do. For example, if you were asked by a playgroup leader for the name of a simple graphics or music program which was suitable for pre-school children (like those in Fig. 5.12), you would probably be able to give some good advice. You would be able to mention the program's good features and point out any difficulties which the children might encounter.

SELLING SOFTWARE

All good salespeople know the strengths and weaknesses of the products which they are trying to sell. When serving a customer, however, they will highlight the good points of their products, and any bad points will either be glossed over or not mentioned at all. Imagine Arthur Daley selling one of his cars. He is likely to be full of enthusiasm for the glossy bodywork, but less forthcoming about the dents in the rear bumper.

Selling a product to a customer is not the same as giving advice to someone you know. If you were asked to sell software to schools in order to make a living, your advice might quickly turn into Arthur Daley sales talk. You would be trying very hard to persuade someone that your product was the best available. If you failed to persuade, you wouldn't make any money, and if you didn't make money, the business would collapse.

When using IT, you will learn:

that each software item has its own strengths and weaknesses, and that the selection of software involves considerations of the facilities offered, ease and simplicity of use, availability and cost

How would YOU go about selling a software package?

Working in groups of around two or three people choose a software package familiar to your group. Imagine that your teacher is a customer who is interested in expanding the school's range of software. Naturally, like any buyer, your teacher will want good value for money. You will therefore need to persuade him or her that what you are offering is the best possible buy for the school.

△ **Fig. 5.14**

SALES PRESENTATION

Your group now needs to consider various key issues before putting together the sales presentation:

- Which areas of the school might the program be used in?
  - Is it a basic IT tool, like a word-processing package, which can be used in any subject, or is the program specifically designed for use in one subject?
- What basic information will the customer want to know?
  - Which software package would suit their needs?
  - Is there an instruction manual?
  - How much does it cost?
- What can the program actually do?
  - If your group has chosen a database, does it print out a variety of graphs?
  - If it is a newspaper program, does it have a variety of fonts?
- How easy or difficult is the program to operate?
- Which IT skills can pupils practise by using the program?

Clearly, as the use of a computer program is a practical activity, you will need to arrange a demonstration as part of your presentation. You will also need to give your customer the chance to ask questions about the program. So part of your preparation will be to anticipate what those questions might be, so that you'll have the right answer ready.

Why not follow this up by composing a jingle to advertise your software? Or you could promote it by making a poster using a DTP program.

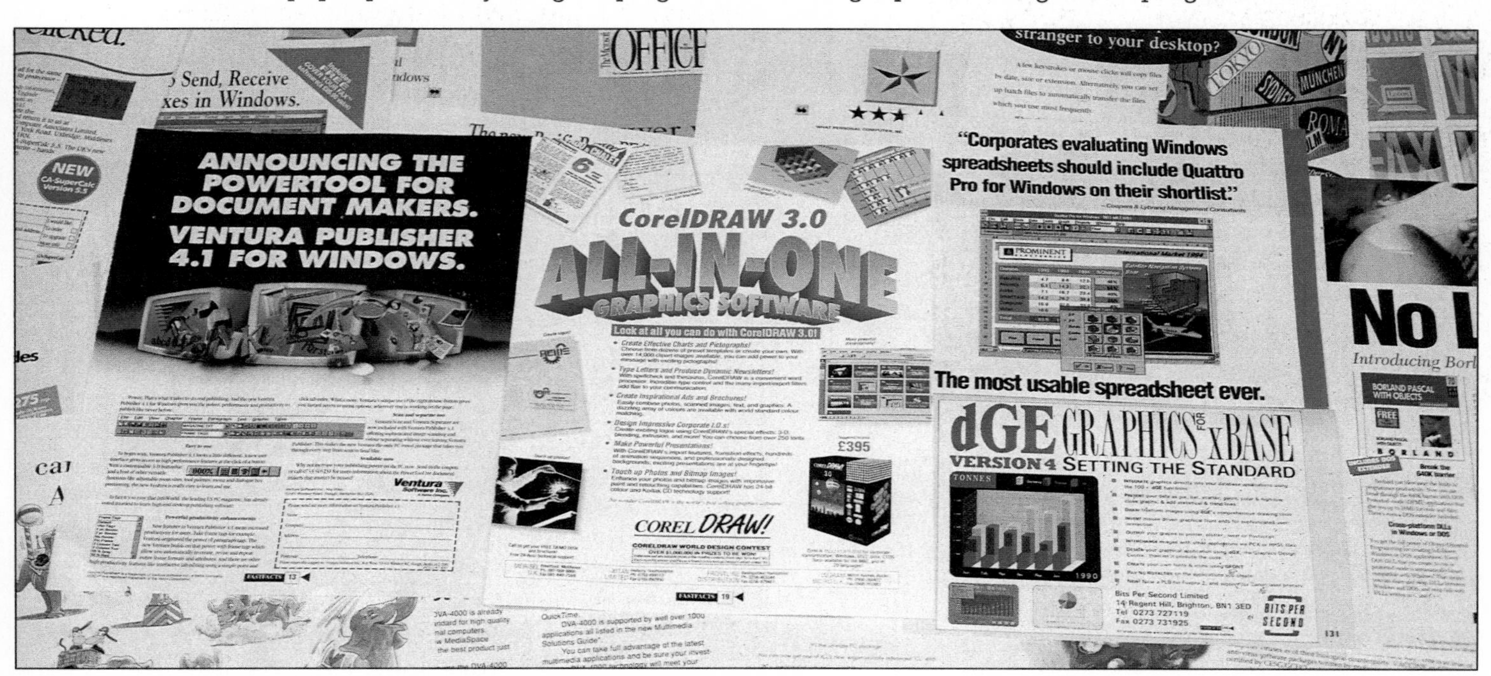

△ **Fig. 5.15 A lot of thought goes into selling software**

Mike Rowchip's OBSESSION

Meet Mike Rowchip. He is a teacher. He has a problem, although he would never admit to it. In fact, Mike doesn't even know that he has a problem. You could drag Mike off to see a doctor, but that wouldn't help at all: his problem doesn't exist in medical textbooks.

Mike's problem is that he has a serious addiction.

HOW IT ALL BEGAN

It all started harmlessly enough when Mike was young. He saw his older sister playing computer games and asked to join in the fun. From that moment he was hooked. He got an Amstrad word processor for Christmas and used it for everything – letters to friends, notes for the milkman, reminders to put the cat out at night. From there, he went on to databases and spreadsheets. Now he was not only communicating with everyone, but also handling vast amounts of information about every aspect of his life.

Little Mikey, aged 5

Mike aged 10 – proud of his work!

FEEDING THE ADDICTION

Unfortunately, Mike's parents made things worse by buying him a simulation program about the oil industry for his birthday. He spent days locked away in his bedroom, lowering the price of petrol at the imaginary garages he was running, calculating, on a spreadsheet, the effect on profits, checking the oil stocks of every country in the world on his database, and word processing letters to explain his price policy.

Mike's bedroom became a shrine to Information Technology. Instead of photographs of his favourite football team, he had video-digitized images on his walls. Rather than posters of pop stars, he stuck up leaflets advertising MIDI interfaces and hand-held scanners.

By the time Mike had left college and started teaching, his interest in Information Technology had become an obsession.

When using IT, you will learn:

that the use of Information Technology does not always provide an appropriate solution to a need, and that effectiveness, appropriateness, and cost of alternative solutions must be considered

Mike's 15th birthday

Mike Rowchip Dip. IT.

'YOU WILL USE IT FOR EVERYTHING'

Imagine Mr Rowchip's delight when Information Technology became part of the National Curriculum just as he started his teaching career. Now he could use all the tools of Information Technology at work, as well as at home.

Mr Rowchip's obsession with Information Technology had made him an expert on the subject. Indeed, those who could follow what he was talking about gained a great deal of knowledge from him. However, in the classroom, his enthusiasm for Information Technology led him to do some very strange things. Here's what happened in Mr Rowchip's lessons:

- He bought a very expensive and powerful database and then wondered how he might use it with the pupils.
- He banned the use of books in project work, saying that books were old-fashioned and that pupils must use only on-line databases and CD-ROMs for finding information.
- He insisted that all pupils should word process their essays and refused to mark anything written by hand.

△ Fig 5.16

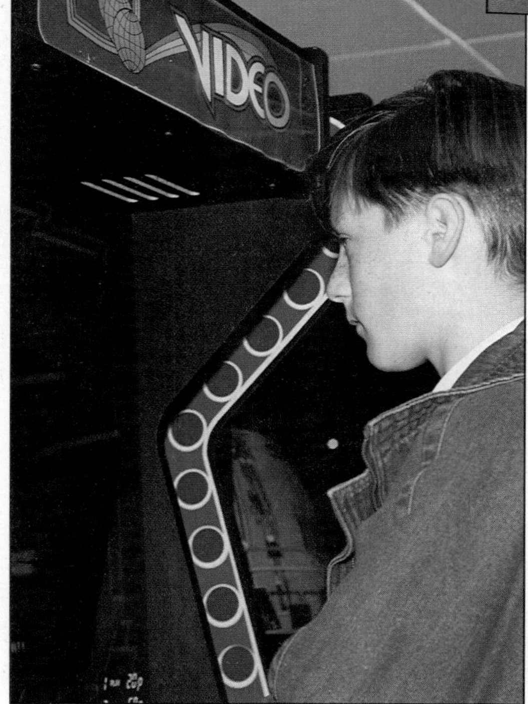

Fig. 5.17 ▷

IT IN MODERATION

Many of Mr Rowchip's pupils disagreed with his ideas about using Information Technology in the classroom. They realized that IT should be used thoughtfully. But there are still many people, especially young people, who become addicted to IT. They can spend all their leisure time playing computer games at home, or, worse still, spending all their pocket-money playing video games in amusement arcades. Using IT in our work can help us to save time, but obsession can have quite the opposite effect. Look at the children in Figs 5.16 and 5.17 – is it a good idea for them to spend *all* their time playing video and computer games? What is *your* opinion of computer addiction? Does it really exist? Do you feel that Mr Rowchip's obsession with Information Technology will be of benefit to his pupils in any way? Do you know anyone like Mike Rowchip?

WORDS FROM THE DEPTHS OF NUMBNESS

In this book, or any other book which discusses ideas about using IT in school, the word 'communication' is used many times. You communicate with the computer by pressing the keys or clicking the mouse, thereby controlling the program. More importantly, you will be communicating with other pupils in your class, explaining your point of view, making plans and responding to the ideas of others.

But what would it be like if you were suddenly stopped from communicating with other people? Imagine the agony of not being able to tell people what you were thinking and feeling; think of the practical difficulties of not even being able to say that you were hungry or cold. Your body would be a prison in which you were kept locked up.

This is not, however, an imaginary situation for some people. People can be born with physical handicaps which prevent them making contact with the world outside their bodies. To make it worse, they sometimes suffer the prejudice of other people who believe that handicap of the body means handicap of the mind.

△ **Fig. 5.18**

THE STORY OF CHRISTOPHER NOLAN

In 1981, a young man called Christopher Nolan struck a blow against such prejudice. He had written a book of poems called *Dam-Burst of Dreams*. Christopher Nolan was only 15 years old, but, even more remarkably, he was born without the ability to control his limbs and seemed unable to communicate. Like many other people, silent throughout the centuries, he was trapped. How had he escaped the prison of silence?

A way was found for Christopher Nolan to make contact with the world. First, he used an electric typewriter with a 'unicorn' stick attached to his forehead which enabled him to depress the keys; he wrote his first poems using this technique. A newspaper article was written about him. This caught the attention of many people who sent him money to buy a computer. It also interested some computer scientists who developed a software program especially for Christopher. Christopher was able to move his head, so a switch was set up which he could strike with his chin. On the computer screen was an alphabet with a cursor hopping between the letters. All Christopher had to do was to move his chin to select the letter when the cursor reached the one he needed. It took him some time to master this program, but it proved to be much easier and quicker than using a typewriter and, as a result, he was able to write two books.

When using IT, you will learn:

to review and discuss your use of IT applications and consider related applications in the outside world and their impact on daily life

THE STORY OF STEPHEN HAWKING

Someone who benefited from IT in a similar way was the cosmologist, Professor Stephen Hawking, the author of *A Brief History of Time*. He had been suffering from motor-neuron disease in which the muscles gradually waste away and movement, including speech, becomes impossible. Stephen Hawking's speech was very slow and difficult to understand, but it was his only means of communication. Then, in 1984, after an operation, he lost his speech entirely. He thought he would be unable to continue with his research, until he received a computer program from California called *Equalizer*. This program is similar to the one used by Christopher Nolan – a switch allows the user to select words from the computer screen to make sentences. Stephen operates the switch by squeezing it in his hand (it can also be activated by a head or eye movement). He can then send his typed sentences into a speech synthesizer which utters them with its simulated voice. This means that he can also use the telephone and give lectures. The computer and synthesizer are attached to his wheelchair so he can now communicate wherever he goes. He recently said
'I can communicate better now than before I lost my voice.'

△ **Fig. 5.19 Children with disabilities learning to use computers**

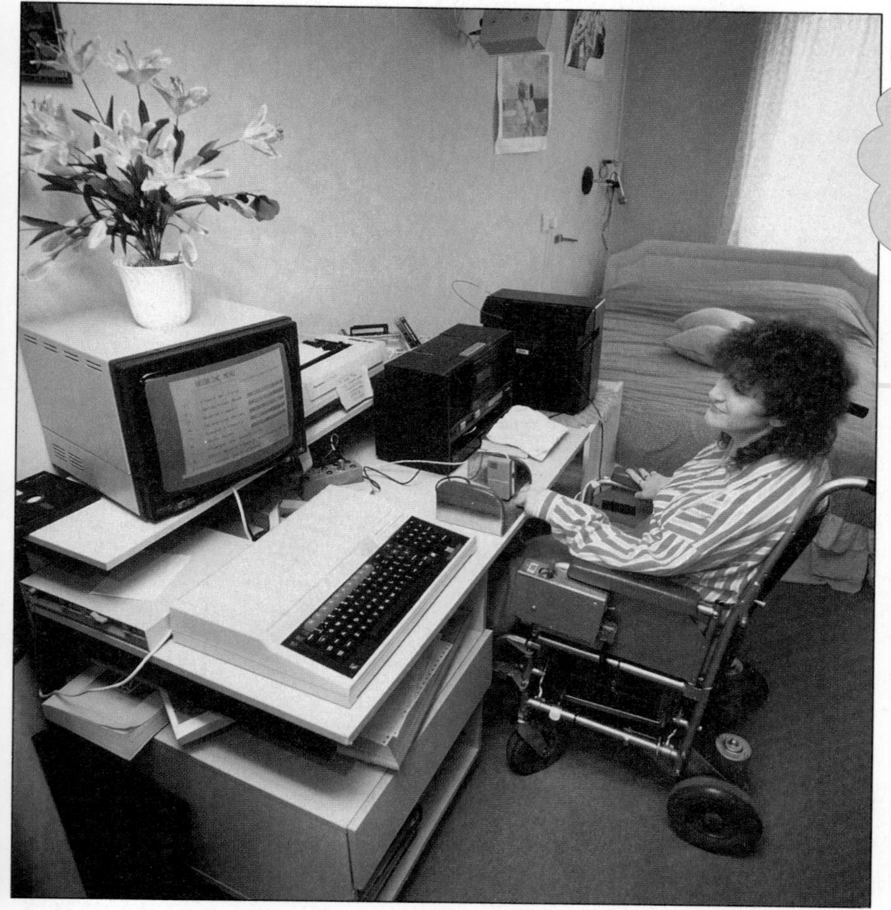

△ **Fig. 5.20 A woman with a disability operating her computer with a pressure pad**

'If computer science can give me a voice, then everyone else who is similarly afflicted stands a chance of being freed.'

– Christopher Nolan

COMPUTER-CREATED FREEDOM

The use of the computer to help people escape from silence is dramatically illustrated in the stories of Christopher Nolan and Stephen Hawking. But in schools and workplaces throughout the country, people who have difficulties in communicating through speech and writing now benefit from computer technology. Both the quality of their lives and the quality of our understanding of their lives have improved.

To improve your own understanding of how Information Technology has helped people with disabilities to communicate, why not visit a school for pupils with moderate or severe learning difficulties to have a look at their work?

ACKNOWLEDGEMENTS

The publishers would like to thank Cathy Burrill for her advice; Sue Morse (London Emblem Plc) for providing badges; D J Cawley (Timestep Electronics Ltd) for providing satellite images; Katy and Alice Bradbury for supplying pupils' handwriting; and John Moyes for the idea of Mike Rowchip. Figure 4.39 and extracts from *Technology in the National Curriculum* and *The Data Protection Act* are reproduced with the permission of the Controller of Her Majesty's Stationery Office. 'About Friends' by Brian Jones from *Spitfire on the Northern Line* is reproduced with the permission of The Bodley Head. The trade directory adverts (p.13) were originally produced by Carres Grammar School, Sleaford.

The publishers would like to thank the following schools for their help with location photography:

Gladesmore Community School, Tottenham (Head of Technology: Cathy Burrill; Teachers: John Burndred, Andy Segal, Peter Whetman; Pupils: Imran Abdulsamad, Negash Admasu, Shamila Bathmanathan, Tommoya Blake, Saranya Boonlertuthai, Medina Christian, Natalie Clarke, Karen Daye, Keffroy Duffus, Ertan Gultekin, Alexander Hadjidemetriou, Hasan Hassan, Joe Hydes, Nural Islam, Lisa Jackson, Michael Jardin, Louise Killing, Abenaa Konadu, Carmen Lupepe, Hayley Marshall, Carley Marston, Rashal Miah, Natalie Mills, Neil Parry, David Paterson, Dilek Ramadan, Dennis Singh, Jagjeet Singh, Malaika Sisulu, Anastasia Stone, Oliver Walker);

William Farr C of E Comprehensive School, Welton (Head of Technology: Mike Finney; Head of Art: Harry French; Librarian: Mrs D L Lee; Pupils: Rebecca Alcock, Sadie Ashton, Kieron Bakewell, Nathan Bray, Sarah Button, Kathryn Clark, Rebecca Cutts, Laura Davey, Joe Donner, Matthew Emerson, Caroline Foley, Rachel Goy, Peter Humphrey, Andrew Jacklin, Michelle Jackson, James Lee, Astrid Marker, Wayne Massey, Matthew McKay, James Morris, Amy Pashley, Jason Phillips, Lisa Phillips, Kelly Rossington, Jamie Smith, Andrew Spalding, Nigel Stephenson, Charlotte Warner, Matthew Watson, Donna Whittle, Richard Williams);

Lionel Primary School, Brentford (Secretary: Jill Benson; Nursery Teacher: Sarah Neno; Pupils: Johnny Guihen, Claire Newman, Sarah Vaughan).

The publishers would like to thank the following for permission to reproduce photographs (the name is followed by the figure number or page number which is followed, where necessary, by (t) top, (b) bottom, (m) middle, (l) left, (r) right):

Anglia Television 2.19; Archiv fur Kunst und Geschichte 2.8; Bantam Press p. 90 (br); Barr Group 4.22; The Bridgeman Art Library 1.25, 1.26; BUPA 2.21, 4.1, 4.16; CAMPUS 2000 2.38; Christie's Colour Library 1.9; Computer Tutorial Sevices Ltd 3.2; Nicola Cornish 1.5, 1.11, 1.15, 1.16, 1.23 (t), 2.25, 2.30, 2.31, 2.32, 2.33, 2.35, 3.12, 3.21, 3.31, 4.19, 4.26, 4.27, 4.38, 5.3 (r), 5.14, 5.15; Driver & Vehicle Licensing Centre 5.8; Alan Edwards 2.23, 2.24, 4.35; Ford Motor Company 4.23; Sally & Richard Greenhill 1.18, 5.12, 5.19; The Health Education Authority 4.17 (words); Michael Horsley 1.6, 1.20, 1.21, 2.5, 2.12, 2.14, 2.15, 2.17, 2.22, 2.27, 3.17, 3.28, 3.30, 4.6, 4.9, 4.12, 4.13, 4.14, 4.15, 4.18, 4.30, 4.36, 4.37; Image Select 1.28; John Groom Association for the Disabled 5.20; The Kobal Collection 2.9; Lloyd's Bank Plc 2.2; London Emblem Plc 2.29; Longman Logotron 1.24, 2.16, 3.26, 3.27, 3.32; Lunn Poly Ltd 5.2; Magnet Trade 3.16 (bl & br); The Mansell Collection 1.10, 1.27, 5.10; ME Company 1.23 (m & b); Malcolm Moyes 2.37; New Home Sewing Machines 3.20; NextBase Ltd 5.3 (l); Mars Confectionery Ltd 4.21; © 1993 Mirror Group Newspapers Distributed by North America Syndicate Inc 4.17 (cartoon); Oracle 2.1, 5.1; Ove Arup Partnership 3.15 (tr & mr); Rex Features 4.7, 5.18; Robert Harding Picture Library 2.6, 2.10, 2.11, 3.34, 4.28; Roy Addison PR and Associates Ltd 5.13; J Sainsbury Plc 3.3, 4.2; Science Photo Library 1.2, 2.13, 3.1, 3.23, 3.24, 4.3, 4.9, 4.20, 4.33, 4.34, 5.5, 5.6; Peter Sharp 1.3, 1.7, 1.8, 1.29, 2.3, 2.4, 2.26, 2.28, 2.36, 3.19, 3.29, 4.5, 4.10, 4.24, 4.25, 5.11; Sherston Software 2.34; Tony Stone Worldwide 3.25; Tropix 5.16, 5.17; John Walmsley 2.18, 2.20; Weidenfeld & Nicolson Ltd p 90 (bl & mr); Zefa 1.1, 2.7, 3.33, 4.31, 4.32, 5.4, 5.7.

GLOSSARY

Automated Library System: an IT system used in libraries to monitor the lending of books and to link up with other libraries.

Backup: a spare copy, usually on a FLOPPY DISK, of a PROGRAM or other DATA.

Bar code: A code made up of thick and thin vertical lines which represent binary numbers. These codes can be found on books and on retail items in supermarkets and contain information regarding the item and its price. Bar codes can be 'read' by a LIGHT PEN or a LASER BAR-CODE SCANNER which transfers the DATA to a COMPUTER.

Buggy: a mechanical trolley, attached to a COMPUTER by a cable, whose movements can be controlled by a PROGRAM.

Byte: a measurement of COMPUTER memory.

CAD (computer-aided design): the use of drawing PROGRAMS as part of the design process. CAD programs produce visual images on the screen which can be altered and manipulated until you are satisfied with your design.

CAM (computer-aided manufacture): the process in which a COMPUTER is directly linked to a machine and actually controls that machine to produce the object that has been designed with the CAD PROGRAM.

Cashpoint: a computerized machine used in high street banks. The user can withdraw money by inputting a personal identification number.

CD-ROM (compact disc read-only memory): a compact disc which stores text, graphics and sound. The amount of information that can be stored is equivalent to around 200,000 pages of typed text. You cannot change or wipe the information on the disc, but you can DOWNLOAD it on to your own disk and then edit it.

CD-ROM drive: *see* DISK DRIVE.

Ceefax: *see* TELETEXT.

Cell: a term used in SPREADSHEET programs to indicate a particular position on that spreadsheet. A cell is located by its column and its row number (e.g. when the CURSOR is in column G and row 14, its position is cell G14). A cell can contain text, numbers or FORMULAS.

Clip art: ready-drawn images that are printed on paper or contained in a piece of SOFTWARE. You can use clip art in your work by scanning the printed images into a COMPUTER, or retrieving the software images from the DISK.

Closed-circuit television: a TV NETWORK, used mainly for security purposes, where a camera transmits pictures to screens by way of cables or telephone lines rather than radio waves.

Computer: an electronic machine that can store, retrieve, sort and manipulate large amounts of DATA at speed, by carrying out a PROGRAM which has been put into it.

CNC (computer numerical control): a type of CAM in which the PROGRAMS used to control the machines are made up of a series of numbers.

Cursor: a marker on the computer screen to show where text will appear when you type. It is often a flashing block or dash, and is sometimes called a 'caret'.

Data: any information, in the form of text, numbers, sounds or graphics, that is entered into, or produced by a COMPUTER.

Database: a store of information on a COMPUTER. *See* DATABASE PROGRAM.

Database program: a type of PROGRAM which provides a structure for the storage of large amounts of information. It organizes DATA into numbered RECORDS, and it allows the user to create and edit DATAFILES and to SEARCH for specific information. *See also* ON-LINE DATABASE.

Datafile: a ready-made DATABASE with information already in it.

Desk-top publishing (DTP): a type of PROGRAM for designing page layouts. Text, pictures and graphics can be moved around and sizes and shapes can be altered in order to achieve the page layout you want.

Digitizer: an electronic device that translates information into a set of numbers that can be read and processed by a COMPUTER. *See also* VIDEO DIGITIZER.

Disk: a means of storing DATA. *See* HARD DISK, FLOPPY DISK, CD-ROM.

Disk drive: the part of the COMPUTER that contains the mechanisms for DISK control. The disk drive spins the disk and reads the DATA on it (like a compact disc player spins and 'reads' the music on a compact disc). It can also copy information to and from disks. The part of the disk drive for FLOPPY DISKS that you can see is the slot in the front of the PROCESSOR. The disk drive for a HARD DISK is also housed inside the processor, but no part of it is visible to you. To read CD-ROM, a computer needs a disk drive that has been specially made for that purpose. A CD-ROM DRIVE, like a floppy disk drive has a slot in the front of it.

Download: to transfer DATA to or from a DISK. This term is often used when the transfer takes place over telephone lines or other remote links.

DTP: *see* DESK-TOP PUBLISHING.

Electronic mail (E-mail): a system for delivering messages by transferring text from one COMPUTER to another along telephone lines.

Facsimile machine (fax): a machine that transmits printed documents down a telephone line. The documents are printed out by the receiving fax machine.

Field: each separate item of a RECORD on a DATABASE. For example, in a phone directory database, each record might have one field for a person's surname, one field for their initials and one field for their phone number. A field can be left empty (i.e. with no DATA in it).

Floor turtle: a computerized self-contained trolley which can be PROGRAMMED to move over a flat surface in response to commands. It is possible to attach a pen to this type of turtle so that it draws a picture as it carries the pen over a piece of paper.

Floppy disk: a thin disk of plastic coated in a magnetic material and contained in a protective plastic casing. It is used to store DATA and must be inserted into a DISK DRIVE for the data to be read or edited. Data can be copied from a HARD DISK on to a floppy disk, which can then be kept separately or used on another COMPUTER . Floppy disks are available in a variety of sizes, most commonly 3.5 inches (which has a rigid plastic case) and 5.25 inches (which has a flexible plastic case).

Font: a particular kind and size of typeface. Most WORD-PROCESSING PROGRAMS have several different fonts. DESK-TOP PUBLISHING PROGRAMS have many more.

Formula: a mathematical equation used in a SPREADSHEET to perform calculations. If a calculation is entered into a CELL as a formula, then the result of that calculation will automatically appear in that cell. For example, to display the total of a column in a particular cell, you could enter a formula to add up all the numbers in that column. If any of the numbers in that column is then changed, the total in the cell which contains the formula will be automatically readjusted.

Graphics: diagrams, drawings, maps, graphs and other images produced on a COMPUTER screen.

Hard disk: a DISK made from rigid material and permanently housed in its DISK DRIVE inside a PROCESSOR. (It can also be in a separate box permanently attached to a COMPUTER.) A hard disk has a larger memory and can store more DATA than a FLOPPY DISK, but the amount of information it can retain is still limited and it may be necessary to remove old data to make space available for new data (the data can be transferred to and stored on floppy disks).

Hardware: the physical parts of a computer system; the parts you can touch. The KEYBOARD, MONITOR, PROCESSOR, DISKS and MOUSE are all examples of hardware, as well as the workings of the system, such as microchips and circuit boards.

Information Technology: a wide-ranging term that encompasses virtually all aspects of computing, data-recording, TV, video and electronic communications.

Input: to enter any item of DATA into a COMPUTER.

Interactive video system: a combination of a COMPUTER and video disc system which allows the user to make choices to control what they see on screen.

Interface: a device that enables a COMPUTER to be connected to another electronic device and allows transmission of information from one to the other. For instance, a computer may work at a much faster rate than the printer it is linked to, so an interface is needed to feed the signals from the computer to the printer at the correct speed and in the correct form.

Keyboard: a piece of HARDWARE for entering DATA into a COMPUTER. It consists of an assembly of keys, like a typewriter, but also has extra keys which perform functions such as SAVING and making text italic.

Keyboard overlay: a strip of paper or printed plastic placed next to or over the keys on a KEYBOARD to show the user what functions these keys perform for a particular PROGRAM.

Key word: a word that, when typed in, the COMPUTER will SEARCH for in a DATABASE or in a piece of WORD-PROCESSED text on the screen.

Label: a term used in SPREADSHEETS that means 'text entered in a CELL'. Labels identify the meaning of the numbers in the relevant columns and rows. For example, in the spreadsheet shown on page 45, 'coffee', 'cornflakes', 'weight' etc. are all labels.

Laser bar-code scanner: a light SENSOR, usually incorporated into a shop counter. When BAR CODES are passed over it, it 'reads' and transfers the DATA contained in the bar code to the COMPUTER.

Light pen: a light SENSOR in the shape of a pen. When it is scanned across a BAR CODE it 'reads' and transfers the DATA contained in the bar code to a COMPUTER.

Logo: a popular computer language designed for schools.

Menu: a list of options which appears on a COMPUTER screen, allowing the users to choose what they want the computer to do. The choices are often numbered so that users can select one by typing the relevant number, or they can highlight their choice using the CURSOR or a pointer controlled by a MOUSE.

MIDI (Musical Instrument Digital Interface): an INTERFACE used to connect a musical instrument with a COMPUTER and enable the transfer of signals in a readable form from one to the other.

Model: a representation, on a COMPUTER, of an object or a situation. A model allows the user to investigate the consequences of actions, without having to experience them in real life.

Modem: a device that links a COMPUTER to a telephone line. Telephone lines are used to connect computers over long distances and modems are needed at each end to convert phone signals into a format that can be read by the computers.

Monitor: the box which contains the COMPUTER screen. It is also known as a Visual Display Unit (VDU).

Mouse: a hand-held device that is connected to the PROCESSOR and is used to move a CURSOR or a pointer around the screen. When a mouse is moved around on a flat surface, the cursor on the screen moves in the same direction. The mouse has a button or buttons on the top of it. When the cursor reaches a certain point on the screen, for example an item on a MENU, the button is pressed to make the selection.

Network: a system that links a number of COMPUTERS together and allows them to share facilities and pass DATA to and from each other.

On-line database: a large commercial DATABASE that is accessed via a telephone and a MODEM. An on-line database is UPDATED by the company that provides all the information. It cannot be altered or updated by the user.

Personal Computer (PC): a COMPUTER that is used by one individual at a time, as opposed to a shared mainframe, where a very large computer is housed in its own room and TERMINALS tap in to it.

Processor: the part of a PERSONAL COMPUTER that contains the microchips, circuitry, DISK DRIVES and any other mechanisms necessary for the computer to function. It is usually a large box, with the MONITOR placed on top.

Program: a set of instructions that are carried out by a COMPUTER. When you use a WORD-PROCESSING PROGRAM, a DATABASE, a SPREADSHEET, etc., the program giving the computer instructions to carry out the relevant tasks has already been written. But you can also write programs yourself, within the ready-written programs.

Record: the parts into which a DATABASE is divided. A database of names and addresses would contain hundreds or even thousands of records – each record would consist of a single name and address.

ROM (read-only memory): COMPUTER memory with DATA that cannot be altered in any way. *See also* CD-ROM.

Save: to store your piece of work on a DISK. Each piece of work must be given a unique name so that it can be found again.

Scanner: an electronic device that copies graphic and textual information from paper into the COMPUTER. A scanner is pulled over an image and sends electrical signals to the computer. These signals are translated into a format that enables the computer to reproduce an exact copy of the original on the screen, which can then be altered by the user and SAVED. Hospitals use a different type of scanner to obtain images of the inside of the human body.

Screen turtle: a CURSOR that can be PROGRAMMED to move around the screen and draw lines to form a picture or a pattern, using a PROGRAM such as LOGO.

Search: a function of DATABASE PROGRAMS and WORD-PROCESSING PROGRAMS. When you use the search function, you type in a KEY WORD which the COMPUTER then searches for, either in a piece of work on screen, or through a whole DATABASE.

Sensor: a device, connected to a COMPUTER, that monitors and reacts to a stimulus (such as light, heat, heartbeat) and inputs DATA directly into the computer.

Simulation: a PROGRAM that allows the users to pretend that they are taking part in a situation which might, in real life, be impossible or too risky for them to participate in.

Software: the parts of a COMPUTER system you cannot touch. The PROGRAMS that control the working of a computer.

Speech synthesizer: a PROGRAM which translates text entered into a COMPUTER into speech-like sounds.

Spreadsheet: a type of PROGRAM which uses rows (horizontal) and columns (vertical) to store and manipulate DATA. A huge amount of data can be stored – a spreadsheet can have around 8,000 rows and 250 columns. Each individual position on a spreadsheet is called a CELL. Text can be entered into a spreadsheet, but the main use is the calculation and recalculation of numbers. Numbers are entered into some cells, then, by using FORMULAS which perform calculations, other cells are automatically filled with totals and results. *See also* LABEL.

Telecommunications: communication of information over long distances.

Teleconferencing: communication between several individuals over long distances by means of a telecommuncations network.

Teleshopping: a method of shopping where products for sale are shown on the television screen. They can be bought by ordering them over the telephone. You don't have to leave your armchair.

Teletext: a system of transmitting information through TV signals. You can see teletext as pages of textual information on your TV screen. The information is UPDATED constantly. The BBC system is called Ceefax, the ITV system is called Teletext.

Terminal: a MONITOR and a KEYBOARD which are connected to a mainframe computer. A terminal does not have its own PROCESSOR.

Text file: a piece of text that is SAVED.

Turtle: *see* FLOOR TURTLE and SCREEN TURTLE.

Update: to amend a DATAFILE or a piece of work that has been SAVED with more recent data.

VDU (visual display unit): see MONITOR.

Video: information in pictorial form on a screen.

Videoconferencing: communication between individuals over long distances whereby each person has a video camera above their TV screen, so the person they are communicating with can see them on their TV screen and vice versa. The screens and cameras are connected by telephone lines.

Viewdata system: a system, similar to TELETEXT, whereby information is sent from a COMPUTER, via a MODEM, by telephone line to another computer. The information is displayed on the user's computer screen.

What if?: a function of a SPREADSHEET which allows the user to try out hypothetical situations and see how that situation affects the DATA.

Word-processing program: a type of PROGRAM that is used to produce documents. Text is typed in and can be easily edited before a perfect, final version is printed out.

Word processor: a loose term for a system using, wholly or mainly, a WORD-PROCESSING PROGRAM.